Grades 4–6

SCIENCE & STORIES

Integrating Science and Literature

From *Science & Stories*, published by GoodYearBooks. Copyright © 1994 Hilarie N. Staton and Tara McCarthy.

Grades 4–6

SCIENCE & STORIES

Integrating Science and Literature

Hilarie N. Staton

Tara McCarthy

Science Advisor: Julie Kane Brinkmann

GoodYearBooks

An Imprint of ScottForesman
A Division of HarperCollinsPublishers

GoodYearBooks

are available for most basic curriculum subjects plus many enrichment areas. For more GoodYearBooks, contact your local bookseller or educational dealer. For a complete catalog with information about other GoodYearBooks, please write:

GoodYearBooks
ScottForesman
1900 East Lake Avenue
Glenview, IL 60025

Book design by Street Level Studio.

ISBN   0-673-36084-9

1 2 3 4 5 6 7 8 9 - ER - 02 01 00 99 98 97 96 95 94

Table of Contents

From *Science & Stories*, published by GoodYearBooks. Copyright © 1994 Hilarie N. Staton and Tara McCarthy.

Making Connections in the Classroom

As you're well aware, teachers of Grades 4 through 6 are under tremendous pressure to cover a great deal of material in key curriculum areas in a restricted amount of time. This book provides ways to make the task easier by connecting and overlapping facets of your science program with facets of your literature and reading instruction, and with other curriculum areas as well.

THE SCIENCE COMPONENT

The time allocated for science instruction increases dramatically as students move out of the primary grades and into grades 4 through 6. For example, many state science curriculums suggest that the 100 to 150 minutes a week allotted in Grades 2 through 4 be beefed up to 250 minutes a week by the time students are in Grade 6. Fortunately, many teachers of Grades 4 through 6 are provided with basal science textbooks and a large array of equipment. The books generally provide students with an abundance of facts, and many suggestions and guides for carrying out hands-on investigations, which access to the equipment facilitates. But many teachers find that the time-strictures, and the textbooks themselves, do not allow enough time for students to manipulate ideas, to discuss and share, or to apply what they're learning to other fields of knowledge and human endeavor.

THE LITERATURE COMPONENT

In many school systems, literature-based curriculums are moving up into the intermediate grades. With these older students, this curriculum usually involves emphasis on the following:

- Reading in content areas

- Studying specific genres of literature, such as biography, myth, nonfiction, fantasy, poetry, and realistic fiction

- Analyzing (and then using in one's own writing) pivotal literary strategies such as development of themes and main ideas, logical presentation of main ideas and supporting details, identifying the audience, presenting a point of view, and describing people, events and phenomena accurately and vividly

INTEGRATING THE SCIENCE AND LITERATURE COMPONENTS

Integrated or theme-based curriculums are already in place and functioning in a few school systems, bringing together skills and concepts from all subject areas and helping teachers develop strategies for combining instruction in two or more heretofore discrete curricular areas, such as geography, science, and math. In this book, we have tried to integrate the science and literature into combined activities that also bring in other subject areas.

1. OBTAINING KNOWLEDGE

Through the activities in this book, students find in different kinds of literature scientific knowledge that supports, supplements, and adds to whatever knowledge they're gleaning through their basal science textbooks and through your science curriculum in general. Students also find their understanding and appreciation of different literary forms and techniques are enriched by the science knowledge they bring to their reading.

2. DEVELOPING PROBLEM-SOLVING SKILLS

Problem solving in science is comprised of four recursive, interacting procedures: brainstorming/questioning, collecting data, analyzing the data, and explaining/applying. These steps probably sound familiar to you, because you already encourage your students to use them as they enjoy and discuss literature. This book suggests explicit strategies for helping students use the procedures as they review the literature, read purposefully for science information, and carry out activities and discussions to help one another analyze data and explain its significance. Students can then go back into the literature to analyze, discuss, and explain how the author integrates science into the book by using a specific genre or specific literary techniques, such as plotting, description, character development, or strong, evocative settings.

3. UNDERSTANDING THE NATURE OF SCIENCE

The nature of science involves its history (its evolution and milestones over time), its philosophy (the assumptions on which it is based and the rules scientists follow), and the interactions of scientists with one another, with the universe, and with technology. The content of much of the literature suggested in this book comes at these understandings directly. Other literature comes at them indirectly, through encouraging students to compare and contrast the nature of science with the nature of different kinds of literature and to analyze and discuss how science and literature work together.

4. FINDING RELATIONSHIPS AMONG SCIENCE, TECHNOLOGY, AND SOCIETY

This component of science instruction becomes increasingly important to students as they proceed through Grades 4-6. Young people not only want to know about our burgeoning technology, but also want to discuss and develop ways to apply it so that it becomes life-enhancing. Fortunately, there is abundant literature, both fiction and nonfiction, for children at these grade levels that shows how human beings and their communities are affected by what scientist discover, by how technology implements the discoveries, and by societal changes wrought by the technology.

HOW WE CHOSE THE LITERATURE FOR THIS BOOK

Out of the hundreds of fine possibilities we considered, we chose literature that met these criteria:

1. The book, whatever its genre, must be exemplary as literature: well written and illustrated, of high interest to young audiences, and representative of a wide range of cultures. In addition, the book must be readily available, either in most libraries or in book stores.

2. The book must not only fit naturally into one of the Unit Themes (Oceans, Change, Ecosystems, Technology, and Space), but also come at that theme in a unique way. That's why each unit suggests books that represent a variety of genres.

3. The book must suggest a variety of related activities in science and literature, including many opportunities for students to discuss, debate, manipulate ideas, work in groups or independently—in sum, to carry out the kinds of interactions and explorations that your traditional science curriculum may not provide time for but that are imperative for producing scientifically responsible, literate students.

From *Science & Stories*, published by GoodYearBooks. Copyright © 1994 Hilarie N. Staton and Tara McCarthy.

4. The selection of books as a whole must take into account the wide range of students' reading abilities at these grade levels. Thus, within each unit you'll find books to challenge your best readers, books for students reading at level, and books for students who need literature that's mature in its concept, but easy to read.

5. Finally, because we believe that sharing literature through reading it aloud together continues to be a powerful binding force in Grade 4-6 classrooms, we've included (with notes to you) several books that definitely suggest this special kind of sharing.

ADDITIONAL MATERIALS

In the Additional Resources Section (pages 130-134), we've listed by unit theme some of the other fine pieces of literature that meet the criteria above. Browsing in libraries and book stores, you'll undoubtedly find other titles that also fill the bill. Encourage your students, too, to find other books they like that tie into the themes or expand upon them. By doing so, they'll be developing their own skill at finding connections between science and literature.

READING-TO-SCIENCE-STRATEGIES

READING STRATEGIES

The following are some of the ways we've incorporated important reading strategies into the lessons.

Modeling thinking processes. Modeling is a monologue that traces your own thinking and decision making. You think out loud to show students how you think. You might model reading strategies or methods for tying fictional literature to science. For instance, in *The Twenty-one Balloons,* you might model how you answer the question for Chapter 2 which asks: From the author's descriptions and the events described, what are some of the properties of hydrogen? Your modeling might proceed like this:

> Let me see how can I figure this out. I know from the first part of the question that the answer will not be given outright. I have to think carefully about what is happening. First, what do I remember about hydrogen from the chapter? They used it to fill the balloons, so it must not be a solid and is probably not a liquid, so it must be a gas. What happened when the balloons were filled? They floated away, so hydrogen must be very light. But it lifted that kid off the ground, so it must be pretty strong or at least a lot of it must fit into a small space.

Teaching reading strategies. Many different reading strategies can be emphasized while reading these lessons. The following are just some suggestions and examples of what can be done:

- Use pre-reading strategies to activate prior knowledge and to learn key science vocabulary before reading. For example, in the Pre-reading section for *Call It Courage,* students recall all they know about the South Pacific and the people who live there.

- Use the cover and title page to recall what you know about a topic. For example, in Ecosystem Lesson 2, students use the cover and title page to identify what they know about the components of a desert ecosystem before reading *Desert Giant,* about the saguaro cactus.

- Use context clues to determine word meaning. Although this can be part of any lesson, many technical words may be unfamiliar to students, so encourage the use of this strategy in the Pre-reading and Connection sections. Questions about context clues and meaning are part of many study guides, such as the one for *The Package in Hyperspace.*

- Read pictures to obtain information. For example, in the Connection activity for *Machines and How They Work,* students must closely examine the pictures for information. Also, the *Magic School Bus* books include a great deal of information in their illustrations.

- Use stories to build specific categories of words. For example, in the lesson for *Lyddie,* students learn about words that describe technology and how it is used in everyday life.

- Use graphs, charts, maps, and diagrams to collect, collate, interpret and categorize information as you read or research. For example, in the Social Studies Connection activity for *Julie of the Wolves,* students create a chart that compares their own culture to that of the Inuit.

- Study a story to find specific information or to identify problems and solutions. For example, the focus of the lesson for *Lyddie* is determining how change created by technology affects people living in a certain society.

- Differentiate between fact and fiction while you read. For example, in *The Package in Hyperspace* students must identify the real science and the make-believe science. They must have a firm background in the science to do this.

- Ask purpose-setting questions before you read. In the Pre-reading activity for *The Magic School Bus on the Ocean Floor,* students are asked two questions to ponder while they read the book.

ORAL LANGUAGE SKILLS

Most lessons incorporate oral language into one or more of the sections. The following are a few of the oral language skills that are suggested.

Listening for specific information. We recommend you read some books aloud to students. In some lessons, discussion questions can be read first so students listen for the answers. Or the questions can be discussed after the pages have been read.

From *Science & Stories,* published by GoodYearBooks. Copyright © 1994 Hilarie N. Staton and Tara McCarthy.

Stretching expressive language. Many of the Extending the Literature activities, such as the activities for *Dragonwings,* invite students to dramatize, do oral readings, or build their descriptive vocabularies.

Oral reading. Choral readings, reader's theater, and storytelling are suggested for several lessons. For example, when myths are studied in the Space unit, the Connection activity includes students choosing one of these ways to retell their story to the class.

WRITING SKILLS

Each lesson has at least one writing activity, and usually more. Some of the skills that are covered in the lessons are:

Informal writing assignments. These might include having students take research notes, keep a journal, or write interview notes. For example, in the activity for *Townsend's Warbler,* students begin a naturalist's journal of their own ecosystem.

Writing process assignments. Students practice the writing process in various lessons. They might work on the pre-writing and organizational skills or carry out ongoing research activities. They use various forms of writing, such as short stories, poems, or radio plays. Editing and revising activities are usually suggested in partner or group situations. Suggestions for sharing or "publishing" their products are often suggested.

Writing to a specific audience. Some assignments invite students to write to a specific audience, such as one activity for the book *Machines and How They Work,* which suggests students describe a machine to a pen pal who has never seen one. These assignments give students a chance to use their knowledge for some specific purpose and to have a reason for keeping an audience in mind.

Descriptive writing. Students are often encouraged to increase their writing vocabulary by identifying and using descriptive words. An activity for the book *City* suggests students rewrite one description they thought was unclear.

IMPLEMENTING MULTILEVEL INSTRUCTION

Multilevel instruction is a new term for what good teachers have been doing all along. They plan interactions and activities that address individual student's strengths and weaknesses and tailor learning objectives to meet individual needs. Here are some suggestions for multilevel adaptations to use with the lessons in this book.

FOR STUDENTS WHO HAVE ACADEMIC OR LEARNING DISABILITIES, YOU MIGHT USE THESE STRATEGIES:

- During reading and oral language activities, ask each question right after students have heard the information. This helps the student who would otherwise have trouble remembering the data.

- For students who have weak receptive language skills, break complex questions (both written and oral) into smaller segments going from concrete information that is easily obtained to the interpretive questions based on that concrete data.

- If students are slower thinkers and speakers, accept accurate answers that are in less complex sentences.

- To help ensure that all students come to school with some prior knowledge, suggest to their families or to support personnel different activities and materials to use with the student before the unit or lesson begins.

- Invite slower students to contribute early in the discussion, before the information they bring to class is co-opted by someone else. If students have trouble drawing conclusions and making predictions during these discussions, amplify the context by using more visuals and help students relate appropriate information to their own experiences.

- Play to the student's strengths. If the student is a good listener, encourage him or her to listen to books on tape or to raise a hand when he or she hears an important idea in a group discussion. If the student is a tactile learner, encourage him or her to manipulate the materials used in the science activities or to design his or her own science activities. For visual learners, use graphic organizers (semantic webs, cycle illustrations, charts, story boards, etc.) to help clarify concepts.

- Give poor readers a chance to practice their reading before oral reading activities. This might be done by pairing a poor reader with a patient, good reader for practice time. Invite other students to read to poor readers if you do not want to emphasize reading skills, but want to emphasize the science concepts.

- Use concrete examples to introduce anything new. For example, in *Journey to the Planets*, students will better remember the relative size of planets when this is expressed in concrete terms, such as a beach ball, a grain of rice, and grapes.

- Accept that some students may not be able to generalize from concrete examples. For example, they may be unable to understand and generalize the dangers of space that face the children in *The Package from Hyperspace*.

- Consider limiting the vocabulary or concepts you expect some students to master. Focus on one or two of the most important terms (such as using only atmosphere and features on the study guide for *Journey to the Planets* and eliminating other, more complex concepts such as axis, rotation, and orbit) and help students master just that concept, asking them to define and apply it where appropriate.

From *Science & Stories*, published by GoodYearBooks. Copyright © 1994 Hilarie N. Staton and Tara McCarthy.

FOR ABLE AND GIFTED STUDENTS, YOU MIGHT USE THE FOLLOWING STRATEGIES:

- Challenge students who are gifted in one or more area to use their skills in different ways. Ask those with cognitive strengths higher-order questions during a science discussion. Invite students with artistic or visual strengths to make charts and other graphic organizers that can be used in class discussions. Suggest students with specialized knowledge share any extra knowledge they have on a particular topic.

- Call on more able students to provide clearer descriptions or definitions. They may also be able to suggest new approaches to scientific, social, or literary problems.

- Occasionally pair a good reader with a poor one. This increases the good reader's self-esteem and can also provide him or her with valuable, mature insights into the learning process.

- While more able students can use their strengths to help the class as a whole, be careful not to always put them in the tutor or researcher roles. From time to time, create a homogeneous group where able students or highly motivated ones can challenge each other to go beyond what the class is doing.

COOPERATIVE LEARNING

In a cooperative learning group, students divide the learning task and then share their knowledge. Each group member is responsible for learning all the material. In this approach, students learn by teaching each other.

Cooperative learning groups are good environments for multilevel modifications. Because these groups are usually heterogeneous, students can be assigned roles that emphasize their strengths or reinforce their weak points. We have suggested a variety of formats for cooperative learning assignments. Other formats can be substituted or added, depending on the social characteristics and skill of your class.

Partner work. This is where students work with one partner to do an activity. This needs the least social sophistication and supplies the most interaction with the content for each student. In the Math Connection activity for *The Green Book,* for example, students work with partners to write math word problems.

Specific roles that come together. In this format, students work at specific jobs that come together as they work. The reading of *The Big Beast Book* is done by groups, in which each student has a role. Then these groups share what they have learned with the entire class.

The jigsaw model. In the jigsaw model, each group member chooses one part of a topic related to the whole. They meet with members from other groups who have chosen the same topic. These "expert groups" research, organize, and fully learn about their topic. This done, they return to their original group and share their expertise with the other group members. Often, this original group must create some product or prove in some way they know the information from each of their expert members.

AUTHENTIC ASSESSMENT

Educators' ideas about assessment have changed considerably in recent years. In classrooms where multiple choice tests once held sway, we now find authentic assessment devices such as portfolios, self-assessment scales, and project evaluations. These strategies are particularly encouraged in the new science curriculums. The emphasis is now on assessing what students have *learned*, not on what has been *taught*. To assess, the teacher must discover *how* and *what* students think about a topic. Many times, students' concepts are not complete. Thus, instruction must be geared to help students complete the concept.

In many lessons, we have included an Evaluation section that helps you identify what to assess and how and when to assess it. This is to make sure students have acquired the necessary science and made the most pertinent connections. This evaluation strategy can be part of class discussions, portfolios, or even individual assessments.

When cooperative learning groups complete a project, you can carry out a complete project assessment by including several components:

a) evaluate the entire product or presentation;

b) evaluate the segment done by each member;

c) ask group members to help you evaluate the processes they used. For example, students can rate how well the group did by answering questions such as Did group members cooperate? Did group members encourage one another? Did group members keep to the subject? It is sometime useful to present scales by which students can assess their cooperative work. For example,

	Always	Sometimes	Never
We kept to the subject.			

The unit opening activities suggest that students keep portfolios throughout each unit. These portfolios not only help students gather information for their final unit synthesis activities, but they can also be used for assessment. Together with the final synthesis activity, the portfolios can show how well the students have connected science and literature and how they have connected overarching concepts. As you know, portfolio assessment is a cooperative procedure between teacher and student. Get the students to tell you their goals, to arrange their portfolios to reflect these goals, to fill in the information or steps they may be missing, and to evaluate their own work.

The final synthesis activity that is suggested for each unit gives you an authentic assessment project for the application of the concepts covered in that unit. For example, the synthesis activity for the Ecosystems unit suggests that students use what they have learned about ecosystems to create an imaginary one. Their ecosystems must reflect some of the relationships students have discovered throughout the unit, such as the relationship between weather and plants or people.

From *Science & Stories*, published by GoodYearBooks. Copyright © 1994 Hilarie N. Staton and Tara McCarthy.

CHARTING AND PLANNING THE SCIENCE AND LITERATURE CONNECTIONS

The chart on the next pages is designed as a quick reference tool with which you can do the following:

a) find a science understanding that fits well with your science unit;

b) find a piece of literature that you can use to enhance or reteach a science understanding or skill;

c) find a science understanding to broaden the literature you've already chosen for your students;

d) find a piece of literature in a specific genre that can also be used to enhance your science program;

e) get an overview of the units, so that you can integrate them into your yearly plans for your whole language classroom;

f) locate activities in other curricular areas such as art, social studies, or music, that you can link to literature or science concepts.

On the chart, the unit and book titles appear in the sequence of the lessons in this book. Within each unit, this sequence was devised so that information and literature flowed from less complex and more concrete to more complex and more abstract. Within the book, the units are not designed to be done in any sequence, but the earlier units do have more activities on a lower level.

Our sequences, both book and unit, aren't set in stone. In fact, it is not even necessary for students to do all the lessons in a single unit. You may just want to use one or two to enhance your science program. Choose the ones that emphasize the most appropriate science subject matter, literature, or activity for your class. Finally, use the chart in conjunction with the Additional Resources on pages 130-134. There you'll find suggestions for other books that can be used in addition to or as replacements for the titles listed on the chart.

From *Science & Stories*, published by GoodYearBooks. Copyright © 1994 Hilarie N. Staton and Tara McCarthy.

THE OCEAN

Students explore the components of the ocean, the interactions of living things within it, and the ocean's importance to humans.

Literature	Genre	Science Problem	Science/Literature Connection Activity	Curricular Links
The Magic School Bus on the Ocean Floor	Fantasy	How does the structure of the ocean affect life in it?	Research various topics relating to the ocean.	Math, Health and Safety
Coral Reef	Nonfiction	How do living things in the ocean depend on one another?	Research and share descriptions of an ocean animal.	Art, Writing
Call It Courage	Legend	How do people depend on the ocean?	Compare character's environment and solutions with own.	Technology, Language
The Turtle Watchers	Realistic fiction	How do we learn about the ocean?	Investigate the life cycle of sea turtles.	Music, Oral Language

PATTERNS OF CHANGE UNIT

Students explore examples of long- and short-term changes that are essential features of the natural world.

Literature	Genre	Science Problem	Science/Literature Connection Activity	Curricular Links
The Big Beast Book: Dinosaurs and How They Got That Way	Reference book	What methods do scientists use to measure time and change?	Investigate and share the work paleontologists do.	Geography, Vocabulary/Art
The Tree	Descriptive writing	What varieties of life have developed over time?	Describe varieties of trees in environment.	Writing, Interviewing
Drylongso	Fiction	What kinds of changes are predictable?	Discriminate among long-term and short-term cycles.	History, Oral Language
The Moon of the Alligators	Nonfiction	How do living things adapt to cyclical changes in their habitat?	Analyze interruptions in the natural food-chain cycle.	Civics, Social Studies, Research
Antelope Woman	Myth	How do human beings both affect change and become affected by it?	Affect a change in your environment.	Writing, Drama

From *Science & Stories*, published by GoodYearBooks. Copyright © 1994 Hilarie N. Staton and Tara McCarthy.

ECOSYSTEMS UNIT

Students explore various ecosystems and how the parts of these systems (including people) interact with and affect other parts of the ecosystem.

Literature	Genre	Science Problem	Science/Literature Connection Activity	Curricular Links
Desert Giant: The World of the Saguaro Cactus	Nonfiction	How is energy recycled in an ecosystem?	Identify life cycles within ecosystem.	Math/Graphs, Social Studies, Art
The Big Wave	Realistic fiction	How do violent forms of energy affect different parts of the ecosystem?	Write nonfiction reports on different aspects of events.	Social Studies, Math
Townsend's Warbler	Biography	How do scientists gather and analyze information about an ecosystem?	Write scientific journals about book's and own ecosystem.	Art, History, Music
The Green Book	Science fiction	How do people adapt to living in a new ecosystem?	Identify problems and alternative solutions.	History, Art, Math
Julie of the Wolves	Realistic fiction	How do changes in one area of an ecosystem affect other areas of the ecosystem?	Investigate how one area of an ecosystem affects the other areas.	Geography/ Social Studies

TECHNOLOGY UNIT

Students explore technology and its relationship to science and society.

Literature	Genre	Science Problem	Science/Literature Connection Activity	Curricular Links
Machines and How They Work	Nonfiction	How do machines use scientific principles and concepts to do work?	Investigate a machine in a variety of ways.	Art, Music, Dance, Social Studies
Dragonwings	Realistic fiction	What methods do people use as they develop new technology?	Identify problems and personal characteristics. which help character pursue scientific inquiry.	Art, Music, Drama, Social Studies
The Twenty-one Balloons	Fantasy	Which scientific principles and concepts are the basis for specific technological devices?	Identify scientific basis and cultural influence of fictional technology.	Geography, Social Studies, Anthropology, Math
City: A Story of Roman Planning and Construction	History	How can technology solve problems that are part of daily life?	Investigate how technology solves society's problems and changes society.	Art, Social Studies
Lyddie	Historical fiction	How can technological changes affect society?	Compare less and more advanced technology in a changing society.	Music, Geography/ Math, Drama, Social Studies

SPACE UNIT

Students explore the night sky, our solar system, and space travel.

Literature	Genre	Science Problem	Science/Literature Connection Activity	Curricular Links
Star Tales: North American Indian Stories About the Stars	Myth	Why does the light of some stars appear brighter than others?	Retell myths and explore scientific concepts and star locations.	Storytelling, Math, History,
Galileo	Biography	How do scientists test ideas? What is the relationship between the Sun, the Earth and the Moon?	Investigate Galileo's life and relate to scientific principles that are known today.	Art/History, Math
Journey to the Planets	Nonfiction	What are the characteristics of the planets in our solar system?	Research individual planets to create comparison visual and essay.	Art, Music, Math
To Space and Back	Personal account	How can people live in space?	Identify components of life during space travel.	Art, Music, Social Studies
The Package in Hyperspace	Science fiction	What unique problems do people have to solve during space travel?	Research the science behind problems of travel in space and suggest a science fiction solution.	Art, Music, Social Studies

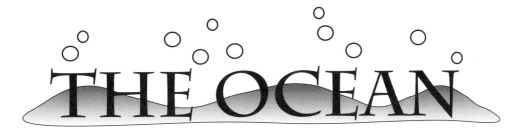

THE OCEAN

SCIENCE UNDERSTANDINGS

In this unit, students explore through literature the components of the ocean, the interactions of living things within it, and the ocean's importance to humans. The unit helps students understand the following concepts from the science curriculum.

1. The ocean contains a large variety of living things, which interact in ways to ensure their survival.

2. Humans depend on the ocean to meet many of their needs.

3. Human knowledge of the ocean is developed through a variety of scientific methods.

Unit Map

Each lesson revolves around a piece of literature, emphasizes a literary genre, and focuses on a problem that students can solve as they work through the lesson.

Lesson	Literature	Genre/Strategy	Problem
1	**The Magic School Bus on the Ocean Floor**	Fantasy	How does the structure of the ocean affect life in it?
2	**Coral Reef**	Nonfiction	How do living things in the ocean depend on one another?
3	**Call It Courage**	Legend	How do people depend on the ocean?
4	**The Turtle Watchers**	Realistic fiction	How do we learn about the ocean?

From *Science & Stories*, published by GoodYearBooks. Copyright © 1994 Hilarie N. Staton and Tara McCarthy.

INTRODUCING THE OCEAN UNIT

1. Show a globe as you discuss how we live on a "water planet." Show how the seas and oceans of the world are connected to form one large ocean. Explain that approximately 70% of the earth is made up of water (97% salt, 3% fresh).

2. Invite students to create a chalkboard list headed *What We Know About the Ocean.* Encourage a wide variety of responses. After the list is completed, suggest that students organize the items on it into categories, such as *Nonliving Things in the Ocean, Living Things in the Ocean,* and *How Humans Use the Ocean.* Ask students to copy each categorized list on a separate sheet of poster paper.

3. Next, ask students to think of questions under the heading *What We Want to Find Out About the Ocean.* Write the questions on the chalkboard. Then have students copy each question in the category where it belongs on their poster-paper lists.

4. Explain that in the books in this unit, students will not only find answers to some of their questions, but will also be able to check or correct many of their "What We Know. . ." statements.

INTRODUCING THE SYNTHESIS ACTIVITY

The synthesis activity gives students an opportunity to apply what they have learned about the ocean through the literature, through related work in your science curriculum, and through further research. Introduce the synthesis activity at the beginning of the units so students can plan ahead.

1. On poster paper, for display, write the objective of the activity:

   Objective: To write an informative book or story about a real island, including data about its formation, the surrounding waters, the life forms in the water and on shore, and the ways in which people of the island use and depend upon the ocean.

2. Explain that the book can be fiction or nonfiction, but that in the former case it should be realistic, not science fiction or fantasy. Tell students that they will be reading examples of fiction and nonfiction as they work through the unit.

3. Suggest that as students work through each lesson, they gather and collate materials that will be helpful to them when they begin to write their books. Portfolio contents can include the lesson Study Guides, additional notes they have made, the results of their work in the extension activities that conclude each lesson, and copies of news clips from periodicals.

4. Explain that students will work in cooperative learning groups to write their books. Students may wish to form these groups at the start of this unit. Groups can come together after each lesson, discuss the contents of members' portfolios, and begin to develop story ideas.

CARRYING OUT THE SYNTHESIS ACTIVITY

Explain the standards you will use for evaluating the books and stories. Write standards on the chalkboard. They might include *accuracy* and *completeness* of facts; *clarity* of presentation; *neatness and accuracy* of visual materials, such as charts, drawings, maps, etc. Encourage students to suggest other standards by which they want to assess their own and their classmates' final products. Remind students to refer often to the Standards list. Reiterate the Objective and ask students to keep it in mind as they develop their stories.

Explain again that each cooperative learning group will be responsible for creating a book. Suggest that students follow these steps.

Step 1. Use maps, the globe, and atlases to determine which island will be the setting of the story.

From *Science & Stories*, published by GoodYearBooks. Copyright © 1994 Hilarie N. Staton and Tara McCarthy.

Step 2. Go through the portfolios to find details that can be used to describe the island and the surrounding waters. List other habitat details the group will need. Assign partners within the group to research and compile these details.

Step 3. As a group, decide whether the book will be fiction or nonfiction. If the book is fiction, decide together on the main characters, plot, key events, and resolution of the story. If the book is nonfiction, decide on the sequence in which facts will be presented.

Step 4. Assign partners to write the fiction chapters or to organize and write sections for the nonfiction book. Assign other members to make illustrations, captions, charts, maps, book covers, and other visuals.

Step 5. Assign two or three group members to act as editors and proofreaders of the group's first draft. Ask each member or partner team to make the corrections for the final draft.

Step 6. Decide on a way of presenting the book to classmates, to students in other classrooms, or to families at home. Invite the school librarian to review the books and suggest ways to share them in a library display. As students enjoy and discuss each other's books, ask them to refer to the evaluative standards and the objective.

INTEGRATION ACTIVITIES

Each lesson concludes with integrating activities to be used with the book students have just read. The following general, ongoing activities will enhance their enjoyment of the unit.

Music of the Sea

Play traditional music of sea-going people around the world. Ask students to listen for common themes and rhythms, as well as for details that are special to a particular ocean environment. To enjoy another kind of music, play some of the many tape recordings of the songs of whales and the whistles and clicks of dolphins. Suggest that students do research to find out what these sounds communicate and what technology is used to capture the sounds on tape.

The Ocean in Art

Most libraries have art books with good quality reproductions of traditional arts and crafts of people who live by the sea. Motifs on fabric, wooden ware, and pottery often have stylized designs of waves, boats, fishes, and ocean birds and mammals. Make such books available to your students. Invite your artists to paint their own abstract designs of ocean life, to mold clay into sea shapes, and to make mobiles that simulate the motion of the sea.

Poems About the Ocean

Have on hand several poetry anthologies that include poems about the ocean. Invite students to find ocean poems and read the poems aloud to a small group of classmates. Some students may also want to write and present their own ocean poems. You might provide some practice time for students to organize a program of ocean poetry, ocean art, and ocean music.

Current Events

Assign a group of students to scan newspapers and news magazines on a regular basis to find news related to the ocean. Ask students to clip out or photocopy articles they think are important and post them on the bulletin board. Or file the clippings in an *Ocean Update* file to place in your science center. Suggest that students append their own notes to tell why they think each article is important or about how it relates to the literature in this unit.

Invite other students to read the articles and comments, then add their own on separate sheets of paper. Two or three times a week, review and discuss the latest additions to the file with the class as a whole. Point out that the file can be a source of ideas to build into the books that cooperative learning groups will be writing.

ADDITIONAL MATERIALS

For additional materials you might want to use with this unit, see Additional Resources, pages 130-134.

LESSON 1

COMPONENTS OF THE OCEAN

LITERATURE:
The Magic School Bus on the Ocean Floor
Joanna Cole (Scholastic, 1992)

SCIENCE UNDERSTANDING:
The ocean contains a large variety of living and nonliving things.

LITERARY GENRE:
Fantasy

BOOK SUMMARY

Like the other books in the *Magic School Bus* series, this volume introduces science facts in a setting of fantasy and humor. Here, the intrepid Ms. Frizzle takes her students step by watery step from the shore to the edge of the continental shelf to the deepest parts of the ocean. Along the way, her students find out about the causes of waves and tides, living things in the intertidal zone, the continental shelf, and the teeming animals and plants along this shelf. Descending to a deeper part of the ocean, the students study cold, plantless, sparsely populated depths where glowing fish get nourishment from waste products and other nutrients that rain from the upper ocean. Moving down, the students examine a hot-water vent, find out how bacteria are manufactured in the vent's heat, and find out why a profusion of life can be supported around these vents. Moving upward again, the students explore the delicate intricacies of coral reefs and the reefs' relationship to undersea volcanoes and to the formation of islands. Back in their classroom, Ms. Frizzle's students—as usual—collate their field trip findings in a giant display.

PRE-READING

This book is fun to read aloud with the entire class. For students who have not yet met Ms. Frizzle and her class in other *Magic School Bus* books, first flip through the pages to point out the many devices for presenting information: straight running text, dialogue balloons, labels, copies of students' reports, inset maps, and pictures. In spite of the slapdash look of some of the pages, the science material is all cognitively related, though some of the children's words are just wisecracks that maintain the light and breezy presentation.

1. Explain to students that along with all the fantasy in the book they will be able to find realistic answers to the following questions. (You might write the questions on the chalkboard.)

   • What are some geographical features of the ocean?

   • How do living things in the ocean get what they need to survive?

2. Distribute copies of the Study Guide. It's a chart, ending with three questions, on which students can take notes as they enjoy and listen to the story. Suggest that students write question marks in chart squares or on

From *Science & Stories*, published by GoodYearBooks. Copyright © 1994 Hilarie N. Staton and Tara McCarthy.

answer lines when they can't guess at the answers. Explain that when they've finished reading, they'll go back into the book and find the answers.

3. Invite students to read along with you in unusual ways. For example, you might read the straight text on each page and invite students to take turns reading the other kinds of text. Ask students who read the dialogue balloons to determine whether the words give scientific data or are just for fun.

BUILDING THE SCIENCE AND LITERATURE CONNECTION

1. When you've finished reading the book, ask students to work with a partner or small group to enrich their Study Guide charts, fill in gaps, and correct errors.

2. When the charts are completed, bring the class together again to discuss and share their chart entries and answers to the questions on the Study Guide. Discuss answers to the two questions in Pre-reading. Suggest that the class refer to the Pre-reading questions and decide if their questions have been answered. Write the answers under the questions. Then have students pose other questions based on what they've read. Remind your class that good science consists not only of answering old questions, but also of coming up with new questions!

3. Ask cooperative learning groups to research and write more fully on some of the topics introduced on the "notebook" pages in The Magic School Bus on the Ocean Floor. Groups might find out more about the vents on the ocean floor and the scientists who discovered them, the plankton and the ocean animals who depend on them, the moon's effect on

tides, or how coral reefs are formed. Have groups present their findings to the class.

4. **Evaluation.** Invite student partners or groups to make up multiple choice tests based on what they learned from The Magic School Bus, using the test at the end of that book as a model. Point out that, as in all good tests, the answer key says not only which answer is right, but also explains why the other answers aren't right. Invite test makers to administer their tests to other groups and discuss the answers.

EXTENDING THE SCIENCE

Activity 1. Suggest that students research and report on the technology for exploring the ocean and its depths. Sample topics might include the 1872 ship Challenger, the Nansen bottle, oceanographic diving, bathyspheres and bathyscaphs, and the NEMO, or Naval Experimental Manned Observatory.

Activity 2. Invite students to research the effects of oil spills and ocean mining on ocean life.

EXTENDING THE LITERATURE

Activity 1. Students can explore point of view in literature by writing a journal entry for one of the characters in The Magic School Bus on the Ocean Floor. For example, students might write a first person entry for Lenny the Lifeguard telling about his reaction to his amazing day with Ms. Frizzle and her class. Or students can take on the point of view of a shark, dolphin, or octopus, telling in the first person how the animal reacted to the sudden appearance in the ocean of a bunch of curious children.

Activity 2. Encourage students to write their own fantasy stories about adventure in the ocean or at the seashore. Suggest that the writers combine fact with their fantasy, using The Magic School Bus as a model. Collect students' journal entries and stories in a folder for your reading table.

OTHER CONNECTIONS
ART: OCEAN SCULPTURE

Have students work in a group to make a tabletop, three-dimensional model of an ocean area. Use plywood as a base and plasticene (a nondrying clay that will hold water) as a liner. Continue using the plasticene to build ocean structures. Encourage students to choose an area of the South Pacific or the Caribbean to show in their model since these are the locales of the next books the class will read. Encourage your model makers to append as many labels and illustrative devices as possible to help viewers understand the model. Keep the model on display for as long as possible. It can be a great device for helping to retell the stories in the upcoming lessons.

HEALTH AND SAFETY IN THE WATER

After reviewing the fantasy elements that allowed Ms. Frizzles's students to go deep-sea diving, invite interested students to write and illustrate real-life safety brochures for people who want to snorkel or scuba. Students can find relevant material at shops that sell the equipment, at tourist and travel agencies, in books about the sports, in travel magazines, and in general encyclopedias. Help students develop categories under which to classify the information they find. Categories might include *Where* to do it, *When* to do it, *How* to check your equipment, *How* to use your equipment, *What* to do if you get into trouble, and *What* you might hope to see.

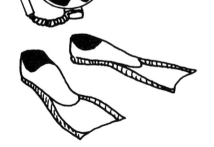

STUDY GUIDE TIPS

1. On the chart, encourage students to write brief notes rather than sentences. For example, under Intertidal Zone, students might write: *sand, rocks; covered by water at high tide; tidal pools at low tide.* Also remind students that they might have to show the pages in the book from which they got their information.

2. In response to questions 1 and 2 at the bottom of the page, students should check and circle all the plants and animals they've listed on their charts.

3. Answers to question 3 and 4 will vary.

From *Science & Stories*, published by GoodYearBooks. Copyright © 1994 Hilarie N. Staton and Tara McCarthy.

The Magic School Bus on the Ocean Floor

Name: _____ Date: _____

DESCRIBING THE OCEAN

Geographical Area: What does it look like?	Plants that live there and how they get nourishment.	Animals that live there and what they eat.
Intertidal Zone:		
Continental Shelf:		
Deep Ocean Floor:		
Hot-Air Vents:		

Analyzing Your Chart

1. Check the items you've listed that depend on the sun.

2. Circle the items you've listed that are part of the food chain.

3. What is the next thing you'd like to learn about the ocean? Why? _____

_____

_____

_____

4. How could you go about learning this?_____

_____

_____

INTERDEPENDENCE OF LIVING THINGS

LITERATURE:
Coral Reef
Jane Burton and Barbara Taylor (Dorling, 1992)

SCIENCE UNDERSTANDING:
Ocean animals interact with one another in ways that promote their survival.

LITERARY GENRE:
Nonfiction science

From *Science & Stories,* published by GoodYearBooks. Copyright © 1994 Hilarie N. Staton and Tara McCarthy.

BOOK SUMMARY

This volume, one in the *Look Closer* series, is outstanding for its organization, its incredible close-up photographs, and its lucid descriptions and examples of how each animal of a coral reef depends upon others. Its fact-packed presentation makes it a good research source for your science curriculum. In addition, the well-written, accurate prose gives students a model to aim for when they are writing about science or about any subject that requires detailed descriptions and explanations.

PRE-READING

1. Review the three student compositions on the pages in *The Magic School Bus on the Ocean Floor,* which tell how a coral reef is built, what coral polyps eat, and what the three main kinds of coral reefs are. Ask students to create a chalkboard list of further questions about coral reefs. Then show the cover and read the title and subtitle of *Coral Reef.* Some students may be able to identify the animals portrayed. Ask students to deduce why these animals are shown (they live in coral reefs), and explain that when they have finished reading the book,

students will be able to identify these animals and many more and to find answers to many of the questions they've listed.

2. Preview the book structure of *Coral Reef.* Show and discuss the table of contents and ask students to predict what animals the book sections tell about. Direct attention to the "Look for us . . ." caption and picture and discuss how realistic presentation of sizes is part of science. (Scientists aim for accuracy and clarity.) Have students skim the index and glossary. Discuss ways in which these are useful to a student of science.

3. Read to students the main copy on the opening pages, "Life on a Coral Reef." Explain that these pages preview each of the animals that will be treated in more depth in the pages that follow. Read two or three of the captions aloud. Explain that the Latin terms in parentheses are the common language of scientists when they are talking and writing about animals and plants.

4. Finally, have students compare and contrast the way information is presented in *Coral Reef* and *The Magic School Bus on the Ocean Floor.* The books are alike in that they use main text, colorful pictures, and captions.

But, from your preview discussions, students should surmise that *Coral Reef,* unlike *The Magic School Bus,* is straight science without the fantasy.

BUILDING THE SCIENCE AND LITERATURE CONNECTION

1. When the class has finished reading the book, distribute the Study Guide and discuss the directions. Make sure each student chooses a subject other than one he or she has read aloud. Conclude the activity by asking students to form groups with different classmates, all of whom have chosen different animals, to share the ideas on their Study Sheets.

2. Discuss the authors' *purpose* for writing about coral reefs and the *method* they use to carry out their purpose. Facilitate the discussion by re-reading the introductory statement on page 8. Most students will understand from this introduction that the authors' purpose is to convince readers that coral reefs should be protected. The *method* used to do this convincing is to give vivid, detailed descriptions of some of the many thousands of animals that depend on the reefs for survival. Ask students to evaluate the authors' purpose and method. Is the purpose worthwhile? Why or why not? Is the method effective?

3. **Evaluation.** Ask students to study the Glossary on page 29. Have them identify words and definitions that describe things necessary to the survival of individual animals or the coral reef itself. Ask students to support their ideas with facts from the book.

EXTENDING THE SCIENCE

Activity 1. Invite a few students to work in a small group to find out where coral reefs occur and draw a map showing the location of major reef areas of the world. Students may wish to draw and label the reefs to identify which are fringing reefs, which are barrier reefs, and which are atolls. As students show their map, ask them to explain why coral reefs form mostly in warm, tropical seas. Display the map. Suggest that students write and post around it other questions they have about coral reefs, then find and post the answers.

Activity 2. Suggest that a group of students study a body of water in your area to find out about the interdependencies and interactions of living things in and around it. Students can use the pages of *Coral Reef* as a model of how to present their findings. Students can contact local, state, and federal water agencies to interview community resource people.

EXTENDING THE LITERATURE

ACTIVITY 1. With the class, develop a list of criteria for good science writing. Suggest that students review *Coral Reef* to get some ideas. Examples of criteria for this genre are clarity, exactness, factual truth, vividness, good examples, clear pictures or other visuals. Good science writers also include indexes and glossaries in their books, and sometimes bibliographies, and lists of additional sources.

Invite students to find and borrow library books and science and natural history periodicals that they think are examples of good science writing. Ask students to tell their classmates about the books and point out how they fill all or most of the criteria the class has developed.

Activity 2. Invite students to contrast and compare the science writing in *Coral Reef* and in *The Magic School Bus on the Ocean Floor* using the four pages in the latter which tell about coral reefs. Ask students to determine, on the basis of what they now know about coral reefs, which components of the School Bus pages present science facts in straight prose (the children's compositions, the labels, some of Ms. Frizzle's instructional remarks) and which present science facts fancifully (the dialogue balloons for coral reef animals). Discuss how each book's approach gets readers interested in coral reefs. Ask students to suggest different audiences for the books or different occasions for using them.

OTHER CONNECTIONS
ART: CORAL REEF MONTAGES

Students can use the photographs in *Coral Reef* as a source of ideas for a paper montage of a reef. In a central location, provide students with colored construction paper, tissue paper and as many other kinds of paper as possible. Students will also need sheets of sturdy paper as backing for the montages, scissors, paste or glue, and colored marking pens.

Encourage students to make some of the shapes for their montages by tearing paper rather than cutting it. This technique is especially effective with tissue paper because it results in soft, flowing lines—appropriate for replicating the motion of the water around the reef and the movement of plants and animals.

Display the montages around the room. Invite students to identify the plants and animals shown and discuss the different ways they are shown in individual work.

CREATIVE WRITING: ANIMAL DIARIES

Invite interested students to imagine they are animals from *Coral Reef.* Have each student choose an animal and write two or three diary entries in which the animal tells (in the first person) about its activities and encounters. Stress that the entries are to give facts but that the writer is free to imagine some fanciful ideas about what the animal is feeling or thinking. Suggest that your writers share finished work with classmates by reading the diary entries aloud, leaving out the name of the animal. At the end of the reading, ask the audience to guess the animal.

STUDY GUIDE TIPS

Have students choose animals on which they have not written or reported. Answers will vary, according to the animal the student chooses. The information required is in *Coral Reef,* though some students might want to do further research outside the book.

Coral Reef

Name:_____ Date:_____

Choose an animal from *Coral Reef.* Draw a picture of it and answer the questions about it.

Name of animal:

_____

1. About how large is the animal?

_____

2. What does it eat?

_____

_____

_____

3. Does it move? If so, how?

_____

_____

_____

4. How does the animal reproduce?

_____

_____

_____

5. How does it protect itself?

_____

_____

_____

HUMAN DEPENDENCE ON THE OCEAN

LITERATURE:
Call It Courage
Armstrong Sperry (Aladdin Books Edition, 1990)

SCIENCE UNDERSTANDING:
Humans depend upon the ocean environment for many of their basic needs.

LITERARY GENRE:
Legend

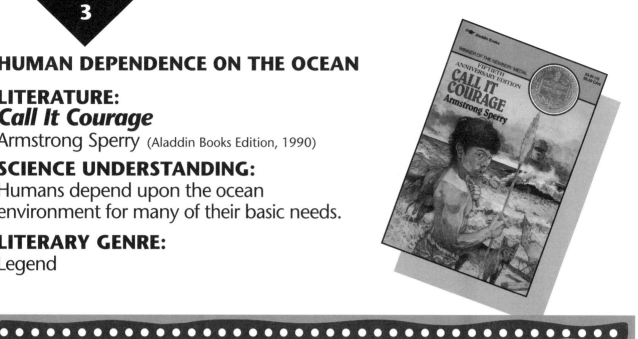

From *Science & Stories*, published by GoodYearBooks. Copyright © 1994 Hilarie N. Staton and Tara McCarthy.

BOOK SUMMARY

A Newbery Medal winner when it was first published in 1940, *Call It Courage* endures as a classic because of its timeless theme of overcoming fear by developing competency. The young protagonist, Mafatu, fears the ocean because of a traumatic event in his infancy. Because he will not venture out on to the ocean, Mafatu is a sore disappointment to his chieftain father, the object of ridicule by his peers, and his own worst critic.

In a burst of desire to resolve this issue by triumph or death, Mafatu undertakes a solo ocean voyage in one of his people's Polynesian longboats. Tossed and shipwrecked by a storm, Mafatu is thrown up on a deserted island far from his home. He learns to use the ocean and the island plants and animals to construct a life for himself. Mafatu's realization that he is a strong and enterprising fellow enables him to return triumphant to his home, where he is celebrated to this day by the people of Hikueru.

PRE-READING

1. As you show the book cover, explain that the story is set in the distant past and is a *legend*,

that is, a story based on events that probably happened, but so long ago that the story has been changed by the storytellers who have handed it down to us. Invite students to discuss the differences between fantasy and legend. Which kind of story do they expect to be more realistic?

2. Ahead of time, orient students to the story's setting and to the main ideas to focus on as they read or listen.

3. On a map or globe, point out the general locale of the story. *Call It Courage* is set in the South Pacific Ocean, south of Hawaii, and north of the Marquesas—a huge territory explored and settled by Polynesian peoples during several centuries before the 1400s.

4. Write the following questions on the chalkboard. Invite students to predict answers and ask them to check their ideas and add to them as they listen to the story.

   • What are some special characteristics of the South Pacific Ocean?
   • How did traditional people of the South Pacific Ocean use the ocean to meet their basic needs?

chalkboard comparison-and-contrast chart like the one below to stimulate discussion and to help groups organize ideas.

	Mafatu	Me
Physical environment		
Social/family environment		
Fear or problem		
Solving the problem		

5. Distribute copies of the Study Guide, discuss its organization, and read the questions. Explain that after they've heard each chapter, students will answer the questions about that chapter. Suggest that students make notes in pencil as they listen to the story. After hearing the story, they'll go back into the book and prepare their final answers.

6. We suggest that you read this story out loud to your class.

BUILDING THE SCIENCE AND LITERATURE CONNECTION

1. After you've read the book out loud, ask students to work with their partners or groups to add to and revise the answers on the Study Guide.

2. When the Study Guides are completed, bring the class together again to share and discuss responses. Where differences of fact or interpretation arise, have students use the book to find details that support their answers.

3. Invite students to form small groups to discuss Mafatu and to relate his problem and his solution to their own lives. You can use a

4. **Evaluation.** Ask student partners to choose one of the two questions you wrote on the chalkboard for Pre-reading. Students should answer the question with an idea web, time line, or chart based on information from *Call It Courage.* Invite students to show and explain their charts to the class.

EXTENDING THE SCIENCE

Activity 1. Have students research and report on one or more of the animals that appear in *Call It Courage.* Among them are sharks, flying fish, bonitos, whales, dolphins, mantas, octopuses, lizards, robber-crabs, albatrosses, parakeets, ghost terns, wild goats, boars, and coral polyps.

Activity 2. Invite students to find out more about currents in the South Pacific Ocean (or another ocean). These are what Mafatu calls *Ara Moana*, the Paths of the Sea. Suggest that students look for facts about the directions of these currents, their influence on weather, how they affect ocean life, and their importance to navigation.

EXTENDING THE LITERATURE

Activity 1. Invite interested student to imagine Mafatu as an adult now, who meets a young person who is as afraid of the sea as he once was. Students can write or dramatize stories in which the grownup Mafatu tells the story of his youthful adventure and helps the young girl or boy conquer his or her fears.

Activity 2. Encourage students to read and report on other books in which people learned how to survive alone in an ocean environment. (See Additional Resources, page 130, for recommended books.)

OTHER CONNECTIONS
TECHNOLOGY: USING MATERIALS CREATIVELY

Suggest that students re-read *Call It Courage* to find how Mafatu and his people used natural resources to make tools, clothes, shelters, and transportation. You might prime the pump by reviewing with students the steps for building a canoe. From the book, your students can find out what materials were used to make not only canoes but also darts, spears, and hooks (whale-bones); clothes (pareu, made from tapa, or mulberry trees); and shelter (coconut fronds). Invite your students to find in the story other examples of creative technology and to tell the class about them.

LANGUAGE: MAKING A GLOSSARY

Invite students to make a glossary of words in *Call It Courage* that would be helpful to another group of students who were approaching the book for the first time. Words can include those from Mafatu's Polynesian language, such as

marae, sacred place; *motu tabu,* Forbidden Island; and *fei,* wild bananas; as well as English words that may need explanation, such as *adze* and *basalt.* Explain that a glossary is arranged alphabetically, includes a definition of each word, and sometimes includes an illustration or sample sentence to further clarify the word's meaning. Ask students to make a cover and put their glossary on a table in your reading center. Encourage students to use the glossary as a reference source as they write about further adventures of Mafatu.

STUDY GUIDE TIPS

Sample answers

Chapter 1: They fish, eat fruits of the island, and build homes of materials there.

Chapter 2: Hazards and challenges include ocean current, winds, storms. sharks, heavy waves, the heat of the sun, and lack of fresh water.

Chapter 3: He'll fish, use the fruit of various kinds of trees, perhaps kill a wild pig. He'll use stones as tools, create fire with sticks, use lime for medicine, and build a canoe from a tree.

Chapter 4: Mafatu meets the challenges of building a shelter and a boat, and of killing animals that threaten him: a shark, a boar, and an octopus.

Chapter 5: Mafatu has learned that the sea is less frightening once you know its ways. About himself, he's learned that he is self-reliant and that he can conquer his fears.

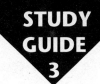

Call It Courage

Name:_____ Date:_____

After you read each chapter, answer the question about it.

Chapter 1: Flight
How do Mafatu's people meet their basic needs?

_____
_____
_____

Chapter 2: The Sea
Describe the hazards and challenges people face in this environment.

_____
_____
_____

Chapter 3: The Island
How does Mafatu use or plan to use available resources in order to survive?

_____
_____
_____

Chapter 4: Drums
What does Mafatu do that makes him feel strong and competent?

_____
_____
_____

Chapter 5: Homeward
What has Mafatu learned about the sea?

_____
_____
_____

What has he learned about himself?

_____
_____
_____

From *Science & Stories*, published by GoodYearBooks. Copyright © 1994 Hilarie N. Staton and Tara McCarthy.

LESSON 4

ACQUIRING AND USING KNOWLEDGE ABOUT THE OCEAN

LITERATURE:
The Turtle Watchers
Pamela Powell (Viking, 1992)

SCIENCE UNDERSTANDING:
Humans can use their knowledge of the ocean in responsible ways.

LITERARY GENRE:
Realistic fiction

BOOK SUMMARY

On the Caribbean island of St. Lucia, three sisters—Esther, Philomena, and Amelia—watch in wonderment one night as a leatherback turtle emerges from the ocean, lays her eggs in the sand, covers them, and returns to the sea. The girls are determined to protect the eggs from people, many of whom consider turtle eggs a gourmet delicacy, and eventually to protect the newly hatched turtles from seabirds and manicous, which try to snatch up the babies as they run from the beach into the sea.

To carry out their mission, the sisters must not only keep the site of the turtle nest a secret from human predators, but also find out about the approximate incubation period of the eggs so that they can be there when they hatch and escort the babies to the ocean. The first goal gets the three girls involved in some high suspense with the greedy turtle hunter Tall Boy and his cohort, a corrupt customs official. The second goal leads them to a rich understanding of the life cycle of the leatherbacks, of the reasons why the species is endangered, and of their own ability to use knowledge to plan and carry out life-enhancing goals.

PRE-READING

1. Ask students to determine from clues in the picture on the book jacket (a) whether the story takes place long ago or in the present (the sisters' clothes, hairstyles, and flashlight indicate the latter), and (b) in what climate region the story is set (palm trees and bare feet indicate the tropics or semitropics).

2. Introduce the story setting. On a detailed map, point out the islands that make up the West Indies and ask students to locate St. Lucia. Ask them to name some of the other islands near it (e.g., Dominica, Grenada).

3. If you have students who come from Caribbean countries, invite them to tell their classmates about the animals and plants of the region, about how people there use these to meet their needs, and about any measures they know of that are being taken to conserve natural resources or to protect certain species. Emphasize to the class as a whole that such firsthand reports are often valuable sources of scientific facts. Explain that the author of this book spent three years in the West Indies researching leatherback turtles with the St. Lucia Naturalist Society.

From *Science & Stories*, published by GoodYearBooks. Copyright © 1994 Hilarie N. Staton and Tara McCarthy.

4. Briefly discuss the book title. On the chalkboard, write *Possible Reasons for Wanting to Watch Turtles* and invite students to suggest some reasons. Ask students to predict what the girls in the jacket-picture might be watching for.

5. As you read the story aloud, pause after each chapter and ask students to predict what will happen in the next chapter. From time to time, discuss what makes the story suspenseful. (the sisters' attempts to stop Tall Boy from finding the eggs; the ominous warnings of Mr. Prentice, the customs official; the mysterious notes, words, and behavior of Old Man Henderson, who may turn out to be friend or a foe to the girls' project; and the overarching, building suspense about when the eggs will hatch and about the sisters' ability to save the babies)

BUILDING THE SCIENCE AND LITERATURE CONNECTION

1. When you've finished reading the book, distribute the Study Guide. Suggest that students work with partners to fill in the idea web, using pencil. Encourage students to use *The Turtle Watchers* as well as reference materials to answer the questions on the web. Bring the class together to share and discuss the drafts of the webs. Then have partners use ideas from the discussion to revise and complete their versions. Suggest that partners make paintings to go with webs. Display the webs and paintings on a bulletin board in your science center.

2. **Evaluation.** Ask small groups of students to review *The Turtle Watchers* to find examples of what methods the sisters used to find out about leatherback turtles (direct observation, research through books, and talking with people who know about the leatherbacks). Suggest that students make charts using the headings above and listing under each heading some facts the heroines learned that way. Bring the class together to discuss finished charts and to discuss how students could use the same strategies to study an animal that is native to your region.

EXTENDING THE SCIENCE
Activity 1. Invite interested students to research and report on sea turtles. Of the seven known species, six can be found in the coastal waters of the United States. Students can organize their findings in charts or displays that show the size and structure of the different turtles, their life cycles, the ways in which they use the ocean habitat to meet their needs, reasons why the turtles are presently endangered, and ways in which humans are seeking to protect the turtles.

Activity 2. Female sea turtles are migrators: they often travel thousands of miles to reach the beaches where they will lay their eggs. Suggest that students research the migratory paths of the leatherbacks, or of other ocean animals, such as humpback whales, which return regularly to the same places to bear their young.

EXTENDING THE LITERATURE
Activity 1. Suggest that students review *The Turtle Watchers* to find details about the home and community in which the sisters live. The book is rich with details about food, house construction, ways of making a living, local music, games, and celebrations. Using encyclopedias and library books, have students find pictures and further descriptions of life in St. Lucia and neighboring islands and report on their findings to the class.

Activity 2. If your students have read *The Magic School Bus on the Ocean Floor,* (see Lesson 1, pp. 4-6) review how that book contains both fact and fantasy. Compare that approach with the realism of *The Turtle Watchers*. Then ask students to think of some ways in which *The Turtle Watchers* could be extended to involve the sisters in a fantasy trip. (For example, the sisters might follow the baby turtles into the sea to track their journey.) Suggest that students write and draw illustrations for such a story to place on a reading table.

OTHER CONNECTIONS
MUSIC: CALYPSO SONGS

Review the calypso lyrics that conclude *The Turtle Watchers*. Explain that calypso is a style of music developed and sung by people of many Caribbean islands, and that a calypso song usually tells about things that are happening currently, all the way from big news events to personal situations. So it's quite natural that the sisters would compose a calypso song about the successful conclusion of their turtle watch. To help students discover the beat and instrumentation of calypso, play a tape of calypso music. Invite students to make up a melody and rhythm for the song in the book.

ORAL LANGUAGE: A RADIO PLAY

Invite students to form a cooperative learning group to write and perform a radio drama based on *The Turtle Watchers*. Group members can review the book, choose key scenes they'll dramatize, and assign speaking roles for story characters. Another important speaking role will be that of the narrator, who introduces the play and links one scene to the next. Three or four students can then write the script, while other group members plan background music and sound effects and set up equipment for taping the play on audiocassettes. The group should also choose a director, who'll help the speakers deliver their lines convincingly and cue the sound technicians.

STUDY GUIDE TIPS

Sample Answers

1. Leatherbacks lay 60-200 eggs at a time in the sands of beaches on the Caribbean islands and South America.

2. The eggs hatch in two to four weeks.

3. The natural enemies of the young turtles are humans, seabirds, land crabs, dogs, fish, and sharks.

4. Leatherbacks are endangered because people hunt then for their meat and for their eggs.

5. Adult leatherbacks live far out in the Caribbean Sea and Atlantic Ocean.

From *Science & Stories*, published by GoodYearBooks. Copyright © 1994 Hilarie N. Staton and Tara McCarthy.

The Turtle Watchers

Name: _____ Date: _____

Answer the questions about leatherback turtles.

1. **Where** do leatherbacks lay their eggs? About how many eggs do they lay at once?

2. **About how long** does it take the eggs to hatch?

4. **Why** are leatherbacks endangered?

3. **What** are the young turtles' natural enemies?

5. **Where** do adult leatherbacks live?

On the back of this page, write two more questions about leatherback turtles. Begin them with **who, what, when, where,** or **why.**

PATTERNS OF CHANGE

SCIENCE UNDERSTANDINGS

In this unit, students explore examples of long- and short-term changes that are essential features of the natural world. The unit helps students understand the following concepts from the intermediate science curriculum.

1. Living and nonliving things change over time.

2. Many changes take place in cycles, or recurring sequences.

3. Large-scale cycles and trends may be irregular or unpredictable in their details.

From *Science & Stories*, published by GoodYearBooks. Copyright © 1994 Hilarie N. Staton and Tara McCarthy.

UNIT MAP

Each lesson revolves around a piece of children's literatur, emphasizes a literary genre or literary strategy, and focuses on a problem students can solve as they work through the lesson.

Lesson	Literature	Genre/Strategy	Problem
1	**The Big Beast Book: Dinosaurs and How They Got That Way**	Reference book	What methods do paleontologists use to measure time and change?
2	**The Tree**	Descriptive writing	What varieties of life have developed over time?
3	**Drylongso**	Fiction	What kinds of changes are predictable?
4	**The Moon of the Alligators**	Nonfiction	How do living things adapt to cyclical changes in their habitats?
5	**Antelope Woman**	Myth	How does knowledge bring about changes in human behavior toward the earth?

INTRODUCING THE PATTERNS OF CHANGE UNIT

1. *Change* is a word with a great many meanings. Invite the class to create a chalkboard list of sentences that contain the word *change*, used as either a noun or a verb. Here are some examples you may wish to use as prompts.

   - I changed my clothes.
   - Her expression changed.
   - The moon seems to change its shape.
   - The shoreline changed after the storm.

2. Focus student attention on the unit theme by asking them to identify the chalkboard sentences that tell about changes scientists study. Underline these sentences. Invite students to suggest what scientists hope to learn by studying these changes.

3. If you plan to have your students carry out the Unit Synthesis Activity (see below), suggest that they start their Patterns of Change portfolios by copying from the chalkboard list two or three of the sentences that tell about the changes that most interest them.

INTRODUCING THE SYNTHESIS ACTIVITY

The synthesis activity gives students an opportunity to apply and present what they have learned about patterns of change through the unit literature, through related work in your science curriculum, and through independent research. If you wish to have your students carry out this project, introduce it to them at the start of the unit, so they will have time to prepare.

1. On poster paper, for display, write the objective of the activity:

   Objective: To create a multimedia presentation that describes and explains a pattern of change in the natural world.

   Explain that to be "multimedia," the presentation should include at least three of the following: written words, spoken words

on audiotapes, live dramatizations or Readers' Theater, video tapes, drawings, photographs, charts or diagrams, live speakers, "surprise" trips, games, or investigations. Students may be able to suggest still other kinds of ingredients for multimedia presentations.

2. Suggest that students use their Patterns of Change portfolios to collect the materials from each lesson. Portfolio contents can include study guides, research notes, and the results of extension activities and integration activities. Also suggest that students categorize and collate portfolio contents according to their own Interest Inventory. The materials that interest them most should appear first in the portfolio. Explain that the "First Place" position may change as students work through the unit.

3. Explain to students that they will be working in cooperative learning groups to plan and present the final product. The groups will be organized as closely as possible around common "First Place" interests of individual students.

CARRYING OUT THE SYNTHESIS ACTIVITY

Form cooperative learning groups by asking students to tell about the patterns of change that interest them most. Team students with classmates who have the same major interest. If one interest (such as the pattern of change in the evolution of dinosaurs) seems to be overriding, two or more groups can work on the same pattern.

Refer students to the project objective, and explain the standards you will use in evaluating the multimedia projects. Write the standards on the chalkboard or on poster paper for groups to refer to as they work. Standards might include the following:

- Accuracy and completeness of facts
- Facts presented in an understandable sequence

- Relevance of each multimedia segment to the main topic
- Neatness of written and drawn materials
- Clarity of words spoken live or on tapes

Encourage students to add to the list other standards by which they want to assess their own and classmates' final products.

Suggest that students follow these steps to create their projects.

Step 1. Go through and share contents of individual portfolios that relate to the pattern of change the group will explicate in its multimedia presentation.

Step 2. Organize the shared materials in a sequence that shows the pattern of change.

Step 3. Decide upon the media that can best show individual steps or trends in the pattern of change.

Step 4. Assign group members to develop the sequential segments, using the medium the group has decided to be most appropriate for the segments.

Step 5. As a group, review and edit the segment drafts to make sure they meet the project objective and the evaluation standards.

Step 6. Practice the presentation you'll give to the class.

Assign a group member to be the narrator. The narrator will introduce the presentation and provide narrative links between the segments.

Step 7. Present your Patterns of Change show to the class. Afterwards, ask your classmates for feedback. What questions do they have? What parts of the presentation did they like best?

INTEGRATION ACTIVITIES
Each lesson concludes with integrating activities to be used with the book students have just read. In addition, these ongoing activities will enhance their enjoyment of the unit as a whole.

WRITING: PERSONAL JOURNALS
Invite students to write daily journals that note changes, large and small, in some natural phenomenon, such as air quality or in some living thing, such as a classroom or household pet. After a student has written several entries, encourage him or her to discern patterns in these changes and note the pattern in the journal. For example, do a hamster's changes in behavior follow a pattern that has to do with food or exercise? Does air quality follow a pattern that has to do with wind, moisture, and temperature? Once the journal writer has identified a pattern, invite him or her to share a hypothesis about the pattern with a group of classmates and devise with them ways to test the hypothesis. Results of these checks become part of the journal too. Emphasize how the keeping of careful records like this is one of the kinds of writing that scientists do.

TRENDS OF CHANGE: LOCAL HISTORY
Invite partners to research, via local historical societies, libraries, and newspaper "morgues" the way your community has changed over the past 100 years. Your researchers can use time lines and copies of old photos to record these changes.

Next challenge students to find out how other communities have changed in the same time period. Which changes show a trend, or are alike, in disparate places? What are the reasons for the similarities? Most of your researchers will identify population growth and new technology as the common factors that make communities in different places change in the same way.

After students present their findings, you might engage the class in a discussion of the positive and negative affects of these trends on human beings and other living things.

From *Science & Stories*, published by GoodYearBooks. Copyright © 1994 Hilarie N. Staton and Tara McCarthy.

READING ABOUT PEOPLE WHO PREDICTED CHANGES

Invite reading partners to find out about the following people, focusing on the changes they predicted in the way human beings think about and use the natural world: Benjamin Banneker, Rachel Carson, George Washington Carver, Albert Einstein, and John Muir. Partners might organize their findings in a chart, with the headings: *Name and Background, Prediction, What Parts of the Prediction Came True?* and *What Can We Learn from This Person's Work?* Display the charts and discuss with the class the data scientists need to collect in order to make valid predictions about changes.

ADDITIONAL MATERIALS

For additional materials you might want to use with this unit, see Additional Resources, pages 130-134.

LESSON 1

STUDYING CHANGES

LITERATURE:
The Big Beast Book: Dinosaurs and How They Got That Way
Jerry Booth (Little, Brown, 1988)

SCIENCE UNDERSTANDING:
Scientists have developed methods for studying how life forms have changed over the course of the earth's history.

LITERARY GENRE:
Reference book

BOOK SUMMARY

This is a reference book with a difference. Not only does the book present the history of dinosaur paleontology and the methods scientists use to date, describe, and reconstruct these animals, but it also invites the young reader to replicate or model scientific methodology to find out exactly how the dinosaur hunters reach their conclusions. Avid dinosaur freaks will want to read the book straight through and try out all the investigations and models. But, like all good reference books, *The Big Beast Book* is also a dip-into-it volume. According to their interests, your students can turn first to any one of the seven chapters to start their study of dinosaurs.

However, most of your students, no matter where they start, will want to flip back and forth to various chapters in this book. With many students, your job will be to help them read the sections they select to study, or to pair one of your top-notch readers with a classmate whose enthusiasm for dinosaurs does not match his or her ability for reading about them.

PRE-READING
1. Many students today know a lot more about dinosaurs than adults do. Help students to focus their prior knowledge on the concept

of patterns of change. Did all the kinds of dinosaurs you know about exist at the same time in Earth's history? (No) Did dinosaurs exist concurrently with human beings? (No) Over what span of time did dinosaurs evolve and change? (150 million years) To help students envision this vast time span, you might use Don Lessem's metaphor from his book *Dinosaurs Rediscovered* (Touchstone, 1993): "Consider that all of life on land began somewhere around your shoulder. Dinosaurs evolved somewhere above your elbow and died out near your wrist. All of human evolution, from beginning to present, is to be found on the tip of your fingernail."

2. Make copies of the Contents page and distribute them to students to refer to as you introduce the book. Read the Introductory page ("Dinosaurs are a problem.") aloud. Then ask students to refer to the Contents page to see how the book is organized (into chapters) to predict the general subject of each chapter, and to find chapter subtitles that particularly intrigue them.

3. Thumb through the book to help students get an idea of its unique design as a reference book: not only does it tell about dinosaurs, but also it asks the reader to do activities to find out more about these animals.

BUILDING THE SCIENCE AND LITERATURE CONNECTION

1. To help students become familiar with the book's approach, read and discuss pages 11-17 with the whole class. Work together on the math problems and carry out the "Striding Through the Millennia" activity. (You'll want to prepare ahead of time for this by getting the sign-making materials together and finding a big, open space where students can do their "striding.") Then skim the rest of the chapter together, concentrating on the subsections that your students find most interesting.

2. Ask students to form six cooperative learning groups. Explain that each group will be responsible for studying one of the remaining six chapters thoroughly, carrying out at least one of the activities in it, and reporting their discoveries and results to the rest of the class. Distribute the Study Guide for groups to use as they read, investigate, and present.

3. Suggest that each group assign these roles to members: two or three "general readers" to read the text aloud to the group, one or two readers to read the dialogue balloons and explain the drawings and picture directions, two or three members to collect the materials needed for the investigation, an "investigation director" to make sure the investigation is being done correctly, two or three scribes to make a final copy of the Study Guide, and a spokesperson to present the conclusions to the class.

4. Give the groups time to present their completed Study Guides to the class and to show the graphics or models that result from their investigation. Suggest that students set up a display table for the graphics, models, and related Study Guides. Invite students to read a chapter another group studied and to do different investigations from that chapter.

5. **Evaluation.** Ask each group to explain how the investigations they did are *scientific.* Students can call on their metacognitive skills in order to explain how they used observation, measurement, testing, drawing conclusions, and verifying. Have them give examples of how paleontologists use these same skills.

EXTENDING THE SCIENCE

Activity 1. If you're fortunate enough to have a natural history museum nearby, take the class to the dinosaur exhibit. Preface the trip by asking the class to develop a list of questions to find answers for at the exhibit. Suggest that each cooperative learning group contribute questions based on the knowledge they've gleaned from their group work. Make photocopies of the class's questions for students to take with them. Discuss where and how they might find the answers at the museum (descriptive labels and paragraphs, audiotaped guides, museum docents, their own observations). Have students note answers on the question sheets you've prepared. Back in the classroom, suggest that each student write a paragraph answering one or two of the questions. Add their paragraphs to the Dinosaur Display table.

Activity 2. Invite a professional geologist or an amateur well versed in geology to help you lead a class trip to an area where students can examine different strata of rock. Possible sites are rock quarries, outcroppings in parks, or cut-throughs near roads and bridges. Ask your resource person to tell about the ages of the different layers of rock, to explain how geologists determine the age, and to use the geological terms for different kinds of rock. Ask students to

take along sketch paper and pencils to record what they see and find out. Suggest that students make finished, labeled drawings to display in the classroom.

Activity 3. Some students may be interested in studying the development and history of other animals that are now extinct, such as mammoths, mastodons, giant sloths, moas, and saber-tooth tigers.

Students studying different animals can get together and construct a time line to show when these animals lived. Ask students to research and read what scientists know or hypothesize about why the animals have disappeared. You can extend the activity by asking students to find out about animals that have very recently become extinct, such as passenger pigeons, or which are in immediate danger of extinction, such as most of the animals living in the world's rain forests.

EXTENDING THE LITERATURE
Activity 1. To help students appreciate that science writing can be a lively art, suggest that they look through *The Big Beast Book* to find paragraphs that strike them as particularly interesting and enjoyable. Ask students to focus on the qualities of these paragraphs such as varied sentence structures (e.g., some short, some long; some questions, some statements), vivid descriptive words and phrases that appeal to the senses, and a clear, accurate sequence of ideas. Invite students to read the paragraphs aloud to classmates and to point out to the audience why the paragraph is a good one.

Activity 2. To help students understand why it's best to use the latest sources when doing science reports, challenge them to find old books about dinosaurs, or entries about dinosaurs in old encyclopedias. Suggest that students look at the copyright dates and find materials published before 1970. Have them compare the "facts" in the old books with the "facts" in newer books about dinosaurs, such as *The Big Beast Book*. While many of the facts will

match up, many others won't. Ask students to make comparison-and-contrast charts of the new and old books. Invite students to share their charts with the class and discuss why the differences exist. Conclude the discussion by asking students if they think that dinosaur books published in the year 2000 will be different from the latest ones they're using now. Why or why not?

OTHER CONNECTIONS
GEOGRAPHY: MAPPING THE BONES
Provide students with large outline maps of the world. Invite them to do research to determine where dinosaur hunters have made and are making their biggest finds. Students should then mark and label these areas on the map. Suggest that students compare and discuss their maps before they make final versions for display.

VOCABULARY/ART: IMPOSSIBLE BEASTS
Students can use the chart on page 43 in *The Big Beast Book* to name, then draw, their own impossible dinosaurs. Remind students that their drawings should incorporate the features that the prefix and suffix identify. For example, a *lalonychus* would have a claw (nychus) that made noises (lalo: babbling). Post the dinosaur drawings and invite students to make up stories about the habits of these imaginary beasts.

STUDY GUIDE TIPS

Invite the class to discuss the last items on the Study Guide to find common difficulties encountered, to share ways of solving them, and to suggest what they might do differently if they undertook the investigations again. Ask groups to post finished copies of their Study Guides in case other groups wish to try the investigations.

From *Science & Stories*, published by GoodYearBooks. Copyright © 1994 Hilarie N. Staton and Tara McCarthy.

The Big Beast Book

Names of group members: _____ Date: _____

_____

Chapter we're studying: _____

A. Here are the five facts we think are most fascinating in the chapter:

_____
_____
_____
_____
_____

B. We did the investigation about:

_____

Here's what we learned:

_____
_____
_____
_____
_____

The most difficult part about the investigation was:

_____
_____
_____
_____

Here's how we solved or dealt with the difficulty:

_____
_____
_____
_____

From *Science & Stories*, published by GoodYearBooks. Copyright © 1994 Hilarie N. Staton and Tara McCarthy.

LESSON 2

VARIETY AMONG LIVING THINGS

LITERATURE:
The Tree
Judy Hindley (Clarkson N. Potter, Inc., 1990)

SCIENCE UNDERSTANDING:
A vast variety of living things has developed over time.

LITERARY GENRE:
Descriptive writing

BOOK SUMMARY

Hindley's brief descriptions of twelve trees include a delineation of their major distinguishing features and a summary of how each tree changes seasonally. This scientific data is incorporated with information about beliefs people have had about each tree and the uses to which the tree has been put through the ages. The prose is lyrical, and can serve as a fine model for your student writers as they learn how to report facts in an interesting way. The author also presents a brief poem about each tree, titled with the tree's "nickname." Alison Wisenfeld's watercolor illustrations echo the prose: they are both accurate and evocative.

PRE-READING

Your students will be studying trees as an example of the variety of life forms that have developed on the earth.

1. Invite students to create a list of all the different kinds of trees they know, in your own area and in other parts of the world. Ask students to note distinguishing features of each tree they name such as the height it attains, the shape of its leaves, the climate it thrives in, the kind of fruit or seed it bears, or the color or texture of its trunk.

2. Discuss how all the trees on the list, different as they may be from one another, share similarities that set them apart from other plants. (a) Most trees continue growing as long as they live, and attain a height of at least 15 to 20 feet. Some ancient trees, like Sequoias, have attained a height of 200 to 300 feet over the thousands of years they have been alive. (b) A tree has one woody stem, called a trunk. This trunk grows to at least three to four inches thick. (c) A tree's trunk can stand by itself.

All other plants are different from trees in at least one of the ways noted above.

3. Introduce the literature by showing the frontispiece of the book. Explain that it shows the leaves of the twelve trees the author describes and discusses. To build observation skills and to set the stage for the author's descriptions, challenge students to describe one of the leaves precisely enough so that classmates can point to the leaf in the picture.

BUILDING THE SCIENCE AND LITERATURE CONNECTION

1. As you read about each tree and examine the illustrations, encourage students to listen for phrases and sentences that they find particularly vivid. ("In the spring, this stiff, little, curly-leaf tree foams with blossom—white or pink or red—as soft as cream." or "Its bark peels away like a curl of paper with a silky lining.")

2. Call your students' attention to the two kinds of change the author deals with in her descriptions. One is the cyclical change in the tree itself over the course of a year. The other change is historical, or linear; the author tells how people once used the tree and what beliefs were attached to it in years gone by. She also mentions some present uses of some of the trees. Ask students to tell which kind of change they personally will be able to observe more (cyclical), and why.

3. By taking a field trip, your students will not only be able to find additional kinds of trees, but also will find the changes, or differences, in varieties of trees from area to area. If possible, arrange to have someone skilled in botany accompany you and your class to help with identification, to explain the optimal conditions for each kind of tree, and to explain the uses of each tree (e.g., lumber, shade, paper, home for animals, medicinal, and so forth). For your field trip, select three sites as different as possible from one another, for example, a river bank or marshland, a woodland or forest, a community park.

Supplies. Student should take with them the following supplies:
- a copy of the Study Guide
- field guides to trees of your region
- sketch paper and pencils
- for making leaf prints: fine, thin paper and a thick, soft pencil
- a folder for carrying all the above

Preparing for the Field Trip. Preface the trip by asking students to form teams of four or five. Go over the Study Guide with the class. Explain that team members are to work together to identify as many as kinds of trees as possible in each area they visit and to enter the names of the trees on the Study Guide.

Data Collection Methods. Team members can share or assign these methods of collecting data:

- Identify each tree by looking it up in the field guide.
- On separate sheets of paper, draw detailed pictures of each kind of tree. Note the name of the tree and where you saw it.
- On the back of each drawing, write a description of the tree. Include details like the ones Hindley did in *The Tree:* the size and color of the leaves, the way the tree trunk feels, the approximate height of the tree, a description of any seeds, fruit, or nuts, the tree bears. (Provide time for students to sit under the trees or to stand for a while and listen to the sound of any breeze or wind in their branches.).
- Make prints (use fallen leaves only) of leaves from trees that you think are particularly beautiful or interesting. To do this, lay the fine drawing paper over the underside of the leaf and rub very gently with the soft-lead pencil. Use the side of the pencil lead, not the point. Label the print with the name of the tree and the location where you found the tree.

4. Back in the classroom, have students discuss the tree distributions shown on their Study Guides. Encourage students to tell why certain kinds of trees grow in certain kinds of habitats and why some areas are heavily treed, while others aren't. One obvious factor is the degree of clearing, building, and development by human beings. Natural factors include the richness of the soil, changing weather patterns, amount of rainfall, and so forth. You may wish to conclude the discussion by having students discuss the importance of trees to life: they release oxygen into the atmosphere, their roots hold soil in place and prevent erosion, and they are the habitats of animals and other plants.

From *Science & Stories*, published by GoodYearBooks. Copyright © 1994 Hilarie N. Staton and Tara McCarthy.

5. As a summarizing and **evaluation strategy,** ask field trip teams to make their own *Tree* books using the materials and information they've collected. Encourage a wide variety of book forms. Some teams may wish to model their pages on those in *The Tree.* Other teams may wish to organize scrapbooks around the three tree sites they've visited. Some teams may enjoy making their book in the form of a mural for class display. Remind students that you'll evaluate their books according to accuracy, good details, understandable organization, and neatness of presentation.

EXTENDING THE SCIENCE

Activity 1. Students who are interested in plants or in the world of the dinosaur may be interested in studying club mosses and horse-tails which, in the days of the dinosaurs, were as tall and as hefty as trees. Indeed, there were no trees then as we know them. The club mosses and horsetails today are quite small but, except for their diminutive size, are just like their ancient ancestors. To get a feel for what a primeval forest was like, students can lie down on the ground and look up through the plants, getting a sort of "ant's eye view" of what it might have been like to walk under those enormous plants.

Students may also extend their study to ferns, the next type of plant to evolve. Suggest that students make a timeline showing big steps in the evolution of plants, from the time of the algae right up to the development of the tree as we know it today.

Activity 2. Suggest that students study trees of the world's rain forests to find out exactly what the consequences will be of destroying these trees. Students can investigate the part the trees play in sustaining entire habitats as well as on the real and potential uses of these trees to make medicines and other products that enhance human life. To inject an up-beat note, ask students to find out about individuals and organizations that are trying to save the rain forests. Suggest that students organize their findings in a three-column chart, with these headings: *How the Rain Forests Are Changing, What Will Happen If the Rain Forests Are Destroyed,* and *What People Can Do To Reverse the Change.*

EXTENDING THE LITERATURE

Activity 1. Invite students to read aloud the poems in *The Tree,* then to make up other poems about trees they studied during their field trip. Invite students to illustrate their poems, read them to the class, then bind them in a folder to place on the reading table. Encourage students to read and discuss the poems with others.

Activity 2. Suggest that students use *The Tree* as a source of entries for a "Picture Glossary of Interesting Words." Students can write, define, and illustrate words like *glossy, scuffle,* and *gnarled,* and write sample sentences using them. Suggest that each glossary entry be on a separate card or sheet of paper, arranged in alphabetical order, and put in a file or folder in your science center. Invite students to add to the glossary whenever they come across a science word that strikes them as especially descriptive or unusual. Suggest that students refer to the glossary when they are writing science reports.

OTHER CONNECTIONS
WRITING: TREE TALES

Within *The Tree,* students can find seeds of story ideas. For example, in the description of the birch tree, readers find out that Native Americans used the birch to construct boats and dwellings. A student might write a story about a young Native American who builds a birch canoe and goes adventuring. Suggest that

From *Science & Stories,* published by GoodYearBooks. Copyright © 1994 Hilarie N. Staton and Tara McCarthy.

your writers read their finished stories to a small group of classmates, then illustrate the stories and put them in a class *Tree Tales* anthology for classmates to read and discuss in their free-reading periods.

ORAL LANGUAGE: FAVORITE TREE INTERVIEWS

Older people often have happy memories of a tree that was special to them in their childhood in environments more rural than the ones most kids know today. There were, for example, birches to swing on, sturdy oaks for climbing, maple trees to build treehouses in, and whole shady groves of trees in which to hold "club meetings." Suggest that students interview residents or visitors in a senior center or senior home to find out about what part trees played in their childhood fun. Suggest that student interviewers use tape recorders (with the interviewee's permission) as a way of taking notes. Remind students to prepare for the interview by making a list of questions that begin with *what, why, where, when, who,* and *how.* Students should phrase additional questions during the interview with these words too.

As a way of sharing the interview results, suggest that students first review their interview notes or tapes with a classmate to identify the most interesting, descriptive responses. Then suggest that the class make a *We Love Trees* mural, collating all their results in a picture montage showing the interviewees as children playing among their favorite trees. Have tape recorders playing the interviews as students study the mural.

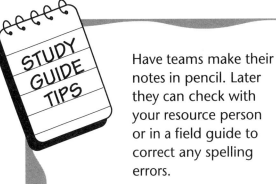

STUDY GUIDE TIPS

Have teams make their notes in pencil. Later they can check with your resource person or in a field guide to correct any spelling errors.

The Tree

Names of team members: _____

Date: _____

Area Visited	Kinds of Trees
FIRST AREA:	
SECOND AREA:	
THIRD AREA:	

From *Science & Stories*, published by GoodYearBooks. Copyright © 1994 Hilarie N. Staton and Tara McCarthy.

From *Science & Stories*, published by GoodYearBooks. Copyright © 1994 Hilarie N. Staton and Tara McCarthy.

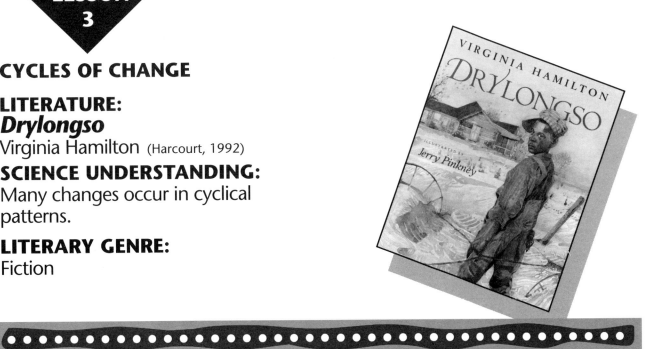

LESSON 3

CYCLES OF CHANGE

LITERATURE:
Drylongso
Virginia Hamilton (Harcourt, 1992)

SCIENCE UNDERSTANDING:
Many changes occur in cyclical patterns.

LITERARY GENRE:
Fiction

BOOK SUMMARY

The time is 1975 and the setting is a farm west of the Mississippi River. Lindy and her parents are farmers. They have been struggling over a three-year-long drought to continue growing whatever meager crops they can and to cope with the personal hardships and privations brought about by a scarcity of water. Now, as they watch an approaching dust storm, they face the ultimate in what dry weather can deal out. But running ahead of this storm is a lad named Drylongso. Lindy and her parents take him in and shelter him.

It soon becomes obvious that Drylongso is not just an ordinary boy. He knows about the cycles of drought and about the farming techniques that deplete the topsoil and make the drought worse. He knows the best times to plant different crops. Most important, Drylongso is a *dowser* and a farming technician: he knows how to find underground springs and how to channel them to create irrigation systems. With Drylongso's help, Lindy's family gets its crops growing again. When the boy leaves, Lindy—and the reader—are left with the sense that Drylongso is both very human, and very much a mysterious, mythic figure.

PRE-READING

1. What annual conditions do farmers count on for growing food crops in your region? Discuss the expected amounts of rainfall and sunshine within the growing cycle of the year, the expected temperatures, and the suitability of the soil for planting and growing crops.

2. From current news reports and from recollections of recent disasters, many students will be able to tell about natural phenomena that interrupt these yearly cycles: unexpectedly cold temperatures, unexpectedly hot temperatures, droughts, and floods. Introduce the book by discussing the jacket illustration and the pictures on pages 7 and 13. Ask students what weather condition they portray. (drought)

Pose these questions: Is it possible that droughts and floods occur in cycles too? If so, do you think the cycles take place over a longer or a shorter period than the usual year-to-year cycle? (longer)

3. Read the author's note on page 55 to your students. Ask them to listen for answers to the following questions:

   • What is the cycle of change that the author tells about?

- Where and when does the story take place?
- What does *drylongso* mean?
- What kind of person do you expect Drylongso to be? In regard to this question, write students' predictions on the chalkboard for them to check out later on.

BUILDING THE SCIENCE AND LITERATURE CONNECTION

1. Because this is an exciting story filled with cliffhangers and a fine development of human relationships, you'll probably want to read the book straight through to your students. However, you might want to pause now and then to briefly discuss the following science concepts and literary insights:

- the drought's long-term effects on families;
- how Lindy and her family make do during the drought years;
- how Lindy's sunny nature and sense of humor lighten the atmosphere;
- the mystery of who Drylongso is and where he comes from;
- Drylongso's observations about plowing and planting. To what extent does he think that farmers are responsible for the lack of crops?
- why Lindy is so anxious to make Drylongso a part of her family.

2. After you finish reading the book, focus students' attention on technology and science by talking about the following:

- Exactly how does Drylongso's technology for planting and watering crops during a drought work? Invite volunteers to draw a diagram on the chalkboard to explain Drylongso's system.
- Drylongso's system for finding underground water is called *dowsing*. Usually, dowsing is done with a willow branch. (If your class has read *The Tree*, students may be able to suggest why the water-loving willow is an appropriate tree for this quest.) Most scientists think dowsing is based on superstition. Many farmers think that no matter what dowsing is based on, it works. Initiate a discussion in which students can talk about how even today scientific knowledge and theory may conflict with folk wisdom. For

example, on page 34 in *Drylongso,* the hero suggest particular times for planting different kinds of seeds. Is this superstition, or is it scientific knowledge gleaned carefully over the years by practitioners of farming?

If you have a *Farmers' Almanac* handy, invite students to browse through it to find signs and rubrics that some farmers follow to predict weather, to note possible changes in normal weather cycles, and to make plans accordingly.

3. Conclude the discussion of the story by inviting the class to make a chart or diagram that shows the normal short-term cycle of the farming year and what weather changes farmers like Lindy's parents expect during this cycle.

4. **Evaluation.** Have students make another chart or diagram that shows the cycle of droughts, as explicated in the story and in the author's note on page 55. Then ask which changes are predictable—the ones on the short-term cycle or the ones on the long-term cycle. (Both are.)

EXTENDING THE SCIENCE

Activity 1. Invite interested students to form teams to research other natural disasters such as volcanic eruptions, tsunami, earthquakes, hurricanes, and floods. Suggest that students focus on these three questions:
- Which of these events happen in cyclical patterns? Explain the cycles.
- What devices or warning signs have people developed to predict major disasters?
- What steps, if any, do people take to protect themselves against possible disasters?

Suggest that students present their findings to the class through an illustrated oral report or chalk-talk.

Activity 2. Invite student partners to research and describe for classmates the differences between changes in weather and changes in climate. Which changes are immediately observable? (weather) Which changes happen over a period of many years? (climate) Suggest

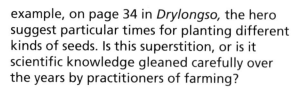

that your researchers make a timeline mural to show changes in the earth's climates over the past million years.

Activity 3. Invite a farmer or other agriculturalist to visit your classroom and tell how farmers today seek to replenish the soil through crop rotation, fertilization, or letting the earth "rest." Suggest that the visitor tell how farmers like those in *Drylongso* make plans to survive long-term cycles that bring about drought.

EXTENDING THE LITERATURE

Activity 1. Invite student to dip back into the book to find the tall tales Drylongso tells about people trapped in dust storms. (pages 26 and 32) Discuss why *Drylongso* told funny stories in the midst of a catastrophe. (to lighten things up) Invite students to make up their own funny tall tales about things that might happen during an earthquake, flood, or other disaster.

Activity 2. Review Lindy's longing for a brother and how this longing is reflected in her feelings about Drylongso. Invite small groups of students to make up story extensions in which Lindy indeed meets Drylongso again. Ask students to read or tell aloud their story extensions to their classmates.

Activity 3. Have students find examples in *Drylongso* of how people cooperated to get work done. Ask students to create lists of other books they've read in which people work together to overcome natural obstacles. Students can find examples in *Sarah, Plain and Tall,* in any of the *Little House* books, in *Caddie Woodlawn,* and even in *Winnie-the-Pooh!* Discuss how a problem makes a good basis for a story. Some of your students may be interested in writing autobiographical accounts of how they, their families, and neighbors worked together in a time of emergency or sudden changes.

OTHER CONNECTIONS
HISTORY: BEFORE THE FARMERS

To help make the point that, for better or worse, humans can bring about changes in established cycles, invite student teams to investigate how land west of the Mississippi was used before the advent of European and African settlers. What plants grew there naturally? What animals thrived in the habitat? How did Native Americans use the land and the living things on it? What changes did the newcomers make? How did these changes affect the life of Native Americans? After students present their reports to the class, you might want to engage your students in a debate about cycles that they think should be interrupted, such as cycles of peace and war, and cycles that they think should not be interrupted, such as the natural cycles that living things follow in their habitats.

ORAL LANGUAGE: BOOK DRAMATIZATIONS

Because *Drylongso* is full of dramatic incidents, strong characters, and opportunities for creative sound effects, you might suggest that a group of students plan and tape a dramatization of the story that would be suitable for a radio broadcast. Use ordinary cassette recorders. Encourage your actors not only to assign the four major roles (Lindy, her mother, her father, and Drylongso), but also to study the characters in order to fully describe them, to assign a narrator for the "bridges" between episodes, and to assign a sound effects crew to simulate the gritty sound of a dust storm, the sound of hoes and shovels hacking into dry earth, and the sound of water bubbling up through underground streams.

Provide your radio actors and sound technicians plenty of time to practice their performance before they tape it, and time to make revisions in the tape. After the radio crew shares the taped play with the class, put the tape in your reading center alongside the book *Drylongso.* Suggest that students listen to the tape as they study the book with a classmate.

From *Science & Stories,* published by GoodYearBooks. Copyright © 1994 Hilarie N. Staton and Tara McCarthy.

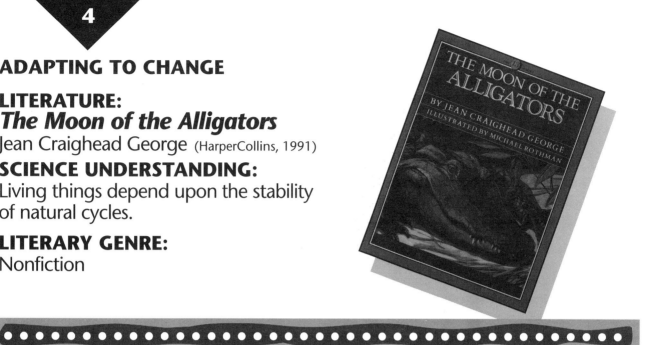

LESSON 4

ADAPTING TO CHANGE

LITERATURE:
The Moon of the Alligators
Jean Craighead George (HarperCollins, 1991)

SCIENCE UNDERSTANDING:
Living things depend upon the stability of natural cycles.

LITERARY GENRE:
Nonfiction

BOOK SUMMARY

This is one in the author's *The Thirteen Moons* series. Each book in the series traces the behavior of a North American animal through the cycle of a year. George begins the alligator's story in "the moon of October," which is the beginning of southern Florida's dry season. It is at about this time that the waters of the great river called the Everglades begin to recede, so that the animals of that habitat gradually seek out the alligator holes as a source of water. Thus ends the long fast of the alligator, which has gone hungry all summer.

Though the pivot point of the story is the alligator's quest for food, the book is actually a narrative description of the Everglades as the habitat of hundreds of different kinds of animals and plants, adapted over thousands of years to the natural cycle of wet and dry seasons. The book explains the near-disaster that has arisen in this delicate ecosystem as humans drained the Everglades for farming and hunters killed tens of thousands of alligators (until legislation declared them a threatened species). The author clearly shows how the alligator, the "farmer" of the Everglades, is a crucial factor in maintaining the balance of life that forms there.

PRE-READING

1. Introduce the book by discussing the jacket illustration and reading the author's preface about the "Thirteen Moons." Focus attention on the last paragraph, and ask students to guess what an animal's "inner clock" is (its instincts for engaging in certain behaviors according to the cycle of the year).

2. Point out the Everglades on a map of the southeastern United States. Then invite students to contribute ideas to a list headed *What I Think the Everglades Is Like.* Post the list and explain that as students read the book they should revise, edit, and add to the list to accommodate what they find out about the Everglades.

3. Ask students to skim the index of *The Moon of the Alligators* and predict why the variety of plants and animals named there are part of a book about alligators. Most students will predict correctly that these living things,

along with the alligator, are part of the Everglades ecosystem. Ask each student to choose two or three items from the index and, as they listen to the story, take special note of how these living things fit into the cycle of life.

BUILDING THE SCIENCE AND LITERATURE CONNECTIONS

1. Because *The Moon of the Alligators* is as exciting and suspenseful as any fiction story, you might want to read it straight through to your class. To make listening purposeful, write the following discussion questions on the chalkboard. Explain that the class will consider and answer them together when you've finished reading the book.

   • What is the natural cycle of weather and water in the Everglades?
   • In what ways is the alligator a farmer and a builder?
   • How do other living things in the Everglades depend upon the alligator to sustain their habitat?
   • What changes did humans make in the Everglades? What happened as a result?

2. As the class answers the questions above, remind individual students to tell particularly how the living things they chose from the book index fit into the natural cycle and were affected by human interference in the cycle.

3. As a summarizing strategy, distribute the Study Guide and ask partners or small groups of students to work together to complete it. Make the book available to students so that they can check out their responses. Bring the class together to review and compare their completed Study Guides.

4. **Evaluation.** Ask students to work with partners to make a chart or diagram that shows the food chain in the Everglades. Again, make the book available to students so that they may find as many individual living things as possible to include in their illustrations.

EXTENDING THE SCIENCE

Activity 1. Many students will be interested in researching and reporting on the visual similarities between alligators and dinosaurs. Suggest that reports include illustrations such as a timeline that shows the development and change in reptiles over the eons, a branching "family tree," or a labeled diagram that shows the similarities and differences between the animals. After your researchers have explained their illustrations to the class, put the pictures in a folder for other students to use as a reference when they are writing or reading about reptiles.

Activity 2. In almost every area of the country, natural ecosystems have been or are being radically changed by humans. Some of your students may be interested in researching such changes in your area. Suggest that these students launch their study and give it direction by first interviewing local wildlife experts and ecologists.

Activity 3. Suggest that students find out what reptiles are native to your area and write and illustrate reports about these animals' natural cycles over the course of a year. Students can work together to make a bulletin board display based on their discoveries.

EXTENDING THE LITERATURE

Activity 1. With a small group of students, discuss how Jean Craighead George builds suspense into the story of the alligator. The most obvious device is the emphasis throughout the book on the animal's hunger: most readers hope that this alligator will find food so that it won't starve to death. Suspense is also created, beginning on page 26, as the alligator dimly recalls an old danger, a place where she "met trouble." Readers wonder what this danger is and hope the alligator won't meet it again. Discuss why the ingredient of suspense keeps readers interested in a story. Students can compare George's story with an encyclopedia entry about alligators. Both book and encyclopedia are accurate, but the suspense in *The Moon of the Alligators* makes the story a "page-turner."

From *Science & Stories*, published by GoodYearBooks. Copyright © 1994 Hilarie N. Staton and Tara McCarthy.

Activity 2. Have students look at the Bibliography on page 47 of *The Moon of the Alligators.* Discuss why writers of nonfiction often include a bibliography at the end of their works (to show some main sources of their information, to suggest further books on the subject that readers might enjoy). Encourage students to include bibliographies in their own science and social studies reports.

OTHER CONNECTIONS
CIVICS: LAWS THAT PROTECT

Review the paragraph on page 14 in which George mentions the Congressional decrees that declared the alligator *endangered,* and later *threatened.* Invite interested students to research the factors that Congress considers before deciding that a living thing falls into either of these categories. Students might want to make and share picture lists of some North American animals and plants that are endangered or threatened.

SOCIAL STUDIES: HOW NATIVE AMERICANS USED THE EVERGLADES

Invite interested students to research the life-ways of the Calusa and Seminole Indians to find out how they to use the Everglades without destroying the ecosystem. Discuss which Native American strategies could be used today, and what obstacles might hinder using these strategies today. The discussion will almost inevitably involve your students in a consideration of conflicting values and goals. This is an opportunity to help students see the difficulties and challenges involved in protecting natural ecosystems while providing for the perceived, changing needs or desires of human beings.

CREATIVE WRITING: ANIMALS WITH "BAD REPS"

Discuss how students' attitudes or beliefs about alligators have changed as a result of reading *The Moon of the Alligators.* Ask students to recall some of the folklore and general misconcep-

tions that have cast the alligator as a "bad guy." Then have students suggest other animals that have bad reputations such as bats, wolves, spiders, snakes, and sharks. Challenge students to find the facts about some of these animals, then write editorials, advertisements, poems, or essays that give a more accurate picture of these animals and celebrate their valuable roles in the ecosystems of which they are a part. After students have shared their work with classmates, hold a general discussion about how changes in attitude are often affected when people have access to facts.

STUDY GUIDE TIPS

On the Season Cycle, students should identify October through April as: natural dry time, humans drain Everglades for irrigation, animals need water, alligator holes are water sources for animals. Students should identify April through October as: natural wet time, animals spread out through Everglades, alligators go hungry. Student responses to the questions should reflect their understanding that:

1. draining the Everglades killed off billions of animals;

2. alligators died off because their food source was depleted and because hunters killed them in large numbers;

3. with the alligators gone, their water holes also disappeared, and thus other animals had no way of surviving through the dry season.

From *Science & Stories*, published by GoodYearBooks. Copyright © 1994 Hilarie N. Staton and Tara McCarthy.

The Moon of the Alligators

Name: _____ Date: _____

A. Write the labels where they belong on the Everglades Season Cycle.

natural wet time

animals spread out through the Everglades

natural dry time

alligators go hungry

humans drain Everglades for irrigation

animals need water

alligator holes are water sources for animals

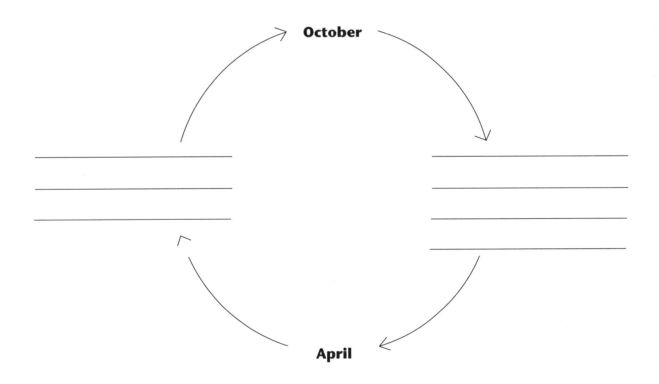

B. Answer these questions on the back of this page.

1. What happened to Everglades animals when humans built canals and drained much of the Everglades?

2. What two human activities caused alligators to begin to die out?

3. When alligator holes disappeared, what happened to other animals in the Everglades? Why?

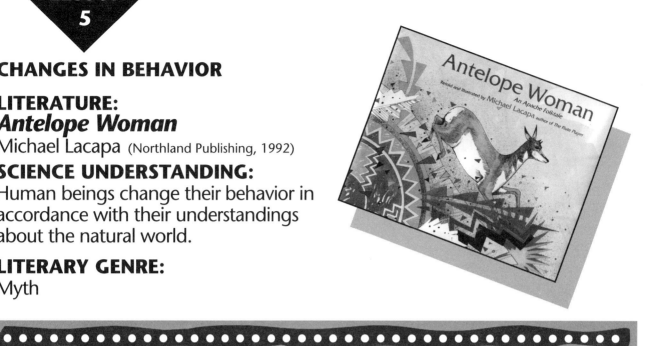

LESSON 5

CHANGES IN BEHAVIOR

LITERATURE:
Antelope Woman
Michael Lacapa (Northland Publishing, 1992)

SCIENCE UNDERSTANDING:
Human beings change their behavior in accordance with their understandings about the natural world.

LITERARY GENRE:
Myth

BOOK SUMMARY

In this story-within-a-story, a father tells his son an ancient legend that explains why his people, the Apache, honor all the living and nonliving things around them.

As the legend has it, there was once a beautiful and capable young woman who had no interest in her many suitors. Then a stranger came to the village and began to teach the people and to help them in such everyday tasks as making hunting bows and carrying water from the stream. The young man ends each lesson by reminding the people to honor all things, both great and small.

Intrigued by this mysterious visitor, the young woman follows him out of the village. At the edge of the woods, the man jumps through four hoops and changes into an antelope. The woman, too, goes through the hoops and is transformed. Living among the antelope people, the woman continues to find many more reasons why it is important to honor all that nature provides. She wishes to return to her human family and share her knowledge with them. The man agrees to go with her, and they return to their human form as they leap through the hoops and go back to the village.

The young couple marries, the man continues his teaching, and in time the woman gives birth to twins. But among the Apache of that time, twins were not accepted into the community, and the young family is shunned. The man convinces his wife that they must return to the antelope people because "they have learned how to honor the family and all things great and small." The wife, her husband, and her children leave the village, pass through the hoops, and are never seen again.

The storyteller concludes by explaining that since that time the Apache have learned to honor all things in nature. In particular, they do not hunt or kill the antelope, for among them are the Antelope Woman and her children, who are part of human life.

PRE-READING

1. Introduce the book by explaining that it is a literary form called a *myth*. Myths are ancient stories that seek to explain how certain phenomena in nature began, or how a people came to have certain values and codes of behavior. Ask students to tell about some of the characteristics of myths they have read such as the "magic" components,

powerful heroes and heroines, and interplay—even the conversations between human beings and other things in the natural world. Suggest that when students listen to *Antelope Woman* they try to identify the qualities that make it a myth.

2. Read students the author profile of Michael Lacapa on the very last page of the book. Then ask where Lacapa finds ideas for his stories. (from the traditional tales told by the Apache, Hopi, and Tewa) Discuss what he means by "the truth found in stories." If myths are full of magic and superhuman deeds, how can they have truth in them? Point out to students that the truth in myths and in many other kinds of stories is in the message they convey. Ask students to also listen for this message as they enjoy the story.

BUILDING THE SCIENCE AND LITERATURE CONNECTION

1. Read the story straight through to students. If you've read the author profile (see 2 in Pre-reading), you might want to allow time for students to study the illustrations and point out the designs and patterns in them that Lacapa found on Southwest baskets and pottery.

2. Invite students to identify the parts of the story that make it a myth. For example, people are transformed into animals and back again; the hero is a mysterious stranger who enters a community and changes people's attitudes toward nature; the story explains the origin of the Apache's special respect for the antelope.

3. Ask students to write statements that identify the truth in this myth. Explain that the truth will be something that seems as sensible and sound today as it was hundreds of years ago for Antelope Woman. Since this truth is repeated often in the story, most students will have no trouble identifying it: "We must honor all things, great and small, in the natural world." Write the statement on the chalkboard.

4. To help students understand how this ancient truth operates in today's world, first discuss the connotations of the word *honor*. It can mean "respect." It can mean "understanding any living thing's vital role in maintaining a habitat or ecosystem." It can also mean "protecting and guarding." Write these ideas, as well as those students contribute, on the chalkboard. Then create a chalkboard list of examples of people and organizations today who honor the living and nonliving things on the earth. Students may not know the exact names, but are likely to come up with general answers such as the following:

   • people who try to stop ships from dumping garbage in the ocean;
   • organizations that are trying to halt the destruction of rain forests;
   • organizations that try to save endangered or threatened animals.

5. Distribute the Study Guide and go over the directions with the class. Suggest that groups complete the Study Guide by following these steps:

Step 1. Decide together on the "honoring" behavior your group will study, such as protecting dolphins.

Step 2. Form two or three teams within the group to use different resources to find out what scientists know about the subject. One team might read recent articles in periodicals, another team might request information from organizations like Greenpeace or The Center for Marine Conservation, and a third team might interview a community resource person who is well-versed in the subject of marine biology.

Step 3. As a group, go through team notes to find the most compelling facts that have convinced many people to behave in an "honoring way" toward this natural entity or situation. Write those facts on the Study Guide.

Step 4. As a group, think of ways in which you might contribute to the effort to honor the life form you're studying. Discuss ideas, choose the ones that are most practical, and write them on the Study Guide.

Step 5. Choose one of your ideas and appoint two or three group members to begin to carry it out. (NOTE: This can be something as simple as making informative posters, or writing informative brochures to distribute to families, neighbors, and students in other classrooms. Depending upon the subject chosen, some groups may wish to launch longer-range efforts by writing letters to local newspaper editors and state and federal representatives, asking for appearances on local TV programs, or organizing and leading clean-up campaigns.)

Step 6. Appoint a group spokesperson to present the group's research and ideas to the class. The spokesperson should encourage the audience to contribute other ideas. Another group member can note these ideas. Later, the group can decide which of them to integrate into the Study Guide.

6. **Evaluation.** Call on students to tell about a new understanding they've gleaned about the natural world, either from *Antelope Woman,* their work in their cooperative learning group, or on their own, and how this understanding may change their behavior.

EXTENDING THE SCIENCE
Activity 1. While Native Americans killed animals and harvested plants for food, they also practiced *husbandry,* the conservation of resources so that ecosystems would not be destroyed and food sources would continue. Invite interested students to explore which hunters today use husbandry. Students may wish to research and compare the food-hunting methods of people like the Inuit, the sport-hunting methods of people who don't need wild animals for food, and the "wildlife management programs" of federal agencies. Use your researchers' findings to spark a debate about which of these groups' strategies the hero and heroine of *Antelope Woman* would consider as "honoring all things, both great and small."

Activity 2. Buffalo were a main food source for Plains Indians. Ask students to research the human behavior that led buffalo to the edge of extinction and to determine from their research why this behavior changed.

Activity 3. Invite interested students to investigate exactly how scientists find out about the natural ways of a wild animal. For example, how do scientists study the natural cycles and behaviors of a wolf or a dolphin without interfering with or changing those cycles and behaviors? Suggest that your researchers use resources available in a library: nonfiction books and periodicals such as *Ranger Rick, Earthwatch,* and *Buzzworm.*

EXTENDING THE LITERATURE
Activity 1. To help students understand how character impels plot, discuss the reason why Antelope Woman found the hero of the story more attractive than any of the other young men that pursued her. (The stranger had wisdom and knowledge that intrigued her, and helpful ways that caught her sympathy.) Then discuss why the hero probably found the young woman attractive. (She was independent, skillful, and adventurous.) Invite students to name other heroines in books they've read who make things happen because they are

From *Science & Stories*, published by GoodYearBooks. Copyright © 1994 Hilarie N. Staton and Tara McCarthy.

curious and adventurous. Examples are Anne in *Anne of Green Gables;* Pippi Longstocking; Caddie Woodlawn, Sarah in *Sarah, Plain and Tall;* and the three sisters in *The Turtle Watchers* (see pages 16-19). Suggest that students make a mural to show heroines like these discovering new things about their world through their adventurousness and curiosity.

Activity 2. Suggest that students find and share other Native American legends and myths that reflect respect for the natural world.

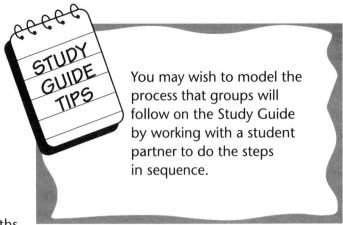

You may wish to model the process that groups will follow on the Study Guide by working with a student partner to do the steps in sequence.

OTHER CONNECTIONS
CREATIVE WRITING: USING MYTHS AS MODELS

Some students might want to use *Antelope Woman* or other myths as models for their own stories about humans interacting with the rest of nature. To help students plan their stories, suggest that as a pre-writing activity, the student confer with a classmate to discuss the main message he or she wants the story to have.

ART: SIGNS AND SYMBOLS

Provide students with books that show pottery, weavings, and baskets made by Indians of the Southwest. Invite students to look for recurring symbols in this artwork and to skim and scan the books to find out the significance of the symbols. Then suggest students incorporate some of the symbols into a piece of art of their own that expresses their feelings about the natural world. Ask students to write captions for their art on index cards. Display the work around the classroom.

From *Science & Stories,* published by GoodYearBooks. Copyright © 1994 Hilarie N. Staton and Tara McCarthy.

Antelope Woman

Names: _____ Date: _____

1. Our group is studying this "honoring behavior":

_____

_____

_____

_____

_____

2. Important facts that prove this behavior honors nature:

_____

_____

_____

_____

_____

3. Ideas about things we can do:

_____

_____

_____

_____

_____

4. We've checked the action above that our group will do. Here are the steps we'll follow:

_____

_____

_____

_____

_____

From *Science & Stories*, published by GoodYearBooks. Copyright © 1994 Hilarie N. Staton and Tara McCarthy.

ECOSYSTEMS

From *Science & Stories*, published by GoodYearBooks. Copyright © 1994 Hilarie N. Staton and Tara McCarthy.

SCIENCE UNDERSTANDINGS

In this unit, students explore various ecosystems and how parts of these systems (including people) interact with other parts. As they explore, students develop the following understandings.

1. When energy enters the ecosystem, it changes the physical environment: energy is used by the living community for growth and activity and eventually leaves the ecosystem.

2. Within an ecosystem, certain materials, such as minerals, water, and gases, are recycled continually.

3. Changes in one part of an ecosystem may affect other parts of the system.

UNIT MAP

Each lesson revolves around one or more pieces of children's literature, emphasizes a literary genre or literary strategy, and focuses on a problem students can solve as they work through the lesson.

Lesson	Literature	Genre/Strategy	Problem
1	**Desert Giant: The World of the Saguaro Cactus**	Nonfiction	How is energy recycled in an ecosystem?
2	**The Big Wave**	Realistic fiction	How do violent forms of energy affect different parts of an ecosystem?
3	**Townsend's Warbler**	Biography	How do scientists gather and analyze information about an ecosystem?
4	**The Green Book**	Science fiction	How do people adapt to living in a new ecosystem?
5	**Julie of the Wolves**	Realistic fiction	How do changes in one area of an ecosystem affect other areas of the ecosystem?

AN INTRODUCTION TO ECOSYSTEMS

1. Discuss the definition of *ecosystem* with students. (a system consisting of a living community that interacts with its physical environment) Encourage them to recall this definition as they do the following activity.

2. Ask students to imagine that they have been assigned to live on a deserted island for three months, with no shipments from the outside. Invite individuals or learning groups to answer the following questions.

   • What would you want to know about your new environment?
   • How would you learn about these things?
   • What do you know you'll need to survive?
   • What do you think you'll need to survive?
   • How would you ensure your survival?
   • What would you like to have with you?
   • What skills will you need?
   • What would you like to find as part of the environment? If it is not available, how would you adapt or improvise?

3. After students have completed their lists, encourage each group to share their answers while you compile a class list. Encourage them to identify the interactions they've suggested with the living community and the physical environment.

INTRODUCING THE SYNTHESIS ACTIVITY

If you plan to do the Final Synthesis Activity, you might want to introduce it to students now to make information from the subsequent activities more pertinent.

1. Write the Final Unit Synthesis Activity Objective (see Final Unit Synthesis Activity) on the chalkboard. Tell students that they will be reading about a variety of real and imaginary ecosystems. As they analyze these ecosystems, they should keep in mind the various components in each ecosystem and how they interact with each other. Also, students should identify how humans adapt and modify each ecosystem, especially by the

use of technology. By analyzing these ecosystems, they will be better prepared to create their own by determining the components and modifications.

2. Suggest that students gather and collate the materials from each lesson into portfolios. The contents of their portfolios can include study guides, research notes, extension activities, and integration activities. The portfolios can be used for reference as students create their own ecosystems.

3. You can also create a chart for students to complete (as individuals, groups, or as a whole class) which summarizes each ecosystem they read about. The chart might include such categories as: land forms, water forms, weather, plants, animals, interactions between physical setting and plants and animals, how humans adapt to their ecosystem, and how humans modify their ecosystem (including technology). Students can meet to fill in and discuss the chart after they finish each book.

CARRYING OUT THE UNIT SYNTHESIS ACTIVITY

This activity allows students to use what they have learned about ecosystems from both your science program and the unit literature to create their own ecosystem. This project can be used to assess knowledge of the basic concepts about ecosystems.

Objective: To create and present an ecosystem with appropriate components, and to show how the components interact with each other and humans.

1. Create several cooperative learning groups. Challenge each group to create a "science fiction" environment where people live. Encourage them to write and illustrate a presentation of their environment. Discuss with students how you will assess the projects.

From *Science & Stories*, published by GoodYearBooks. Copyright © 1994 Hilarie N. Staton and Tara McCarthy.

2. Suggest students follow these steps to create their project. These steps can be put onto a classroom chart or worksheet for the students to refer to during their projects.

Step 1. Have students list these details of their environments: physical setting, such as land and water forms and weather; plants and animals that are adapted to the physical setting; interactions between plants, animals, and the physical setting; how humans adapt to and modify the ecosystem, including their use of technology.

Step 2. Draw a picture or diagram of the environment and choose the details that best describe it. Add words, phrases, and descriptions that label parts of the environment.

Step 3. Decide and plan the presentation. Think of events, dialogue, and conflicts that will add to the reader's knowledge of your environment. List ways the environment could affect the action or change a character.

Step 4. Use your lists to develop a plot. Include events where the ecosystem is a critical factor. Sequence your events.

Step 5. Create the presentation. Be sure each group member has an important role in creating the final product.

Step 6. Practice and edit your presentation until it is in final form.

Step 7. Make the presentation to the class.

Suggest that groups divide the tasks so that all members contribute to the final project and its presentation. Allow the groups ample time to complete their environments and then ample time to share them. Encourage other groups to analyze and evaluate each presentation.

INTEGRATION ACTIVITIES
These activities can be done while the students are reading any of the books or after they have completed them. They connect the general unit theme to other content areas in especially creative ways.

MUSIC/POETRY CONNECTION
Locate music that was written to describe a certain natural location like "Night on Bald Mountain" or "Grand Canyon Suite." Play the music for students without telling them the title. Invite each student to write a list of descriptive words the music makes them think of. Emphasize that every person will have a different list. Suggest each student share their list with two other students. Encourage them to add words to their personal list that they especially like. Invite each student to write a poem describing the place they visualize, using their word lists. You may want to suggest they use specific poetic forms, such as haiku or cinquains. Invite students to illustrate their poem and share them with the class. Combine the poems into a class poetry book.

GEOGRAPHY CONNECTION
Invite individuals or groups to create a topographical, weather, or other special map that relates to one particular environment. After they research the type of map, students can use both fiction and nonfiction sources for the data (i.e., weather systems, altitudes, populations). Encourage students to display their completed maps in class.

WRITING CONNECTION
Invite students to choose a favorite descriptive passage of a place from a book and then to rewrite the description as a different type of author might. They might choose to rewrite it as a scientist writing an observation journal, a tourist writing a letter, or a poet writing a poem. Invite them to share their writing with other students in class.

ART CONNECTION
Students can use elements of the environment they are studying to create a collage. The collage doesn't need to show the place, but can represent it in texture, tone, or impact. A student studying the Eastern woodlands might

use dirt, leaves, twigs, and nuts, while a student studying a swamp might include flowers, fur, olive green paper (for murky water), and moss.

ADDITIONAL MATERIALS
For additional materials you might want to use with this unit, see Additional Resources, pages 130-134.

From *Science & Stories*, published by GoodYearBooks. Copyright © 1994 Hilarie N. Staton and Tara McCarthy.

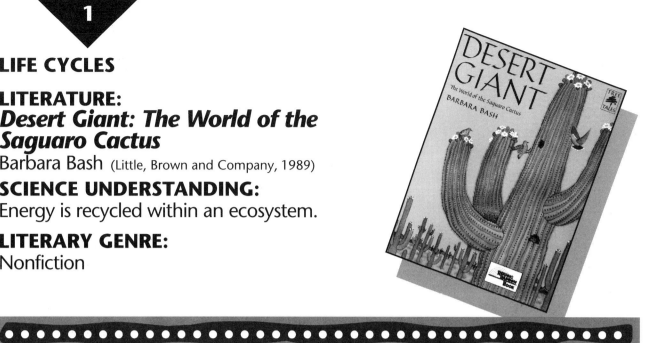

LESSON 1

LIFE CYCLES

LITERATURE:
Desert Giant: The World of the Saguaro Cactus
Barbara Bash (Little, Brown and Company, 1989)

SCIENCE UNDERSTANDING:
Energy is recycled within an ecosystem.

LITERARY GENRE:
Nonfiction

BOOK SUMMARY

This clear, simple, nonfiction book tells the story of the saguaro cactus and its ecosystem. It describes the physical adaptations that have enabled the saguaro cactus to survive in the desert, and the animals that depend on it. The Gila woodpecker pecks a nest in the cactus flesh and the cactus forms a callous lining around that hole. That lining remains after the cactus decomposes. The Indians use these linings to make "saguaro boots." The elf owl and hawks also nest in this cactus. When the cactus blooms, bats, doves, bees, and butterflies pollinate the flowers on their one day of life. The fruit of the cactus is enjoyed by the Tohono Indians, who harvest it each June and make jams, candies, syrup, and wine. Birds, lizards, even coyotes and wild pigs come to enjoy the fruit. When the saguaro cactus dies, it provides a home and food to other creatures: insects, lizards, snakes, and mice. Young saguaro cacti have many obstacles to overcome as they grow into plants. They need the protection of a nurse plant, as they grow slowly and don't produce flowers or fruit until they are fifty years old. Their arms don't develop until they are seventy-five or older. Many live to be a hundred and fifty.

PRE-READING

Begin with the unit introductory activity on page 46 to introduce students to survival in an ecosystem. Review the definition of an *ecosystem* (a system consisting of a living community that interacts with its physical environment).

1. Invite students to discuss what a plant needs to survive. (sun, nutrients, water) Review or teach about photosynthesis so that students understand that the sun provides the energy for plants to make their own food.

2. To activate prior knowledge and set the purpose for reading, display the cover and title page of the book. Encourage students to identify the type of ecosystem (desert) and general components of desert ecosystems.

3. Write the following three questions on the chalkboard or on a poster. Invite small groups or pairs to use their knowledge about deserts and cacti to predict the answers.

   • What is the ecosystem of the saguaro cactus like?

- What does the saguaro cactus need to survive?
- How does the saguaro cactus interact with other living things to help them survive?

BUILDING THE SCIENCE AND LITERATURE CONNECTION

1. Distribute the Study Guide, which illustrates the life cycle of a saguaro cactus. Discuss how the page is organized and what type of information students need to add to it (i.e., the animals that make their homes in the cactus). Encourage students to take notes on the back of the page while they read or listen to the book being read.

2. After students have completed the Study Guide, discuss the information they've included and how this information helps them understand more about the saguaro cactus and its place in the desert ecosystem.

3. Invite the small pre-reading groups to evaluate their predictions. Encourage them to change their answers to fit what they have learned from the book.

4. Divide the class into small cooperative learning groups. Invite each group to choose a different living thing from the saguaro's desert ecosystem. Suggest that each group investigate two questions about their organism: What does it need to survive in the desert ecosystem? and What is its life cycle? Invite each group to share their findings with the class.

5. **Evaluation.** Gather student together to create a class mural of the saguaro cactus's desert ecosystem. Have each student write or tell a "life cycle story" using the class mural.

EXTENDING THE SCIENCE
Activity 1. Students can research and illustrate several food webs of the desert. Some food webs should include the saguaro cactus These food webs can be shared on a desert bulletin board.

Activity 2.
Students might enjoy researching and illustrating food webs and life cycles for plants and animals within their local ecosystems. The information for their food webs and life cycles can come from observation as well as reference sources. Students can create presentations with their visuals to give to younger classes which are studying your local area.

Activity 3. Advanced or interested students might like to research the characteristics that place succulent plants into a separate classification from the other plants they encounter daily. They can design long term studies to see what affect variables such as water, light, and temperature have on each type of plant. They can also look at leaf sections of each type of plant under a microscope. Finally, they create a classification system of at least two categories (succulent and nonsucculent plants) and the characteristics they've chosen for each. As a final evaluation, encourage students to classify several unknown plants using the criteria they have created.

EXTENDING THE LITERATURE
Activity. Have each student or group imagine a desert journey and write a journal that includes observations of the desert ecosystem. Students can include what they saw, how they felt, and what they thought. Encourage them to use figurative language to make their descriptions vivid and to share their observations with the class.

RECOMMENDED READING
Students can read poetry books, such as *Mohave* by Diane Siebert or *Desert Voices* by Byrd Baylor, which are specifically about the

From *Science & Stories*, published by GoodYearBooks. Copyright © 1994 Hilarie N. Staton and Tara McCarthy.

desert. Invite students to use what they have learned about desert life and figurative language to write their own poems and to share them with their class.

OTHER CONNECTIONS
MATH/GRAPHS

Invite students to research the average life span of the saguaro cactus and other living things. The assignment can be limited to the desert ecosystem if you have enough available resources. If not, encourage students to use living things within their own environment. Create a class bar graph comparing their information. Pairs of students can create word problems that require the use of the graph. They can trade problems with another pair of students or add them to a math activity center.

SOCIAL STUDIES/CULTURES

Invite students to investigate the cultures of desert dwellers. Students might choose the Tohono O'odham Indians from the book, or the Pueblo or Navaho of the U.S. Southwest. If you are studying foreign cultures, encourage students to investigate the people who live in or near the Sahara, Gobi, or other deserts. Encourage students to identify ways these people adapt to the desert environment and what they use from it in order to survive.

STUDY GUIDE TIPS

Throughout the book, students will find a variety of ways to describe the cactus at the four stages depicted, and many examples of ways in which the cactus is used. Ask students to be prepared to show the book pages on which they found the information. The next-to-last page tells about threats to the saguaro seeds, seedlings, and young plants.

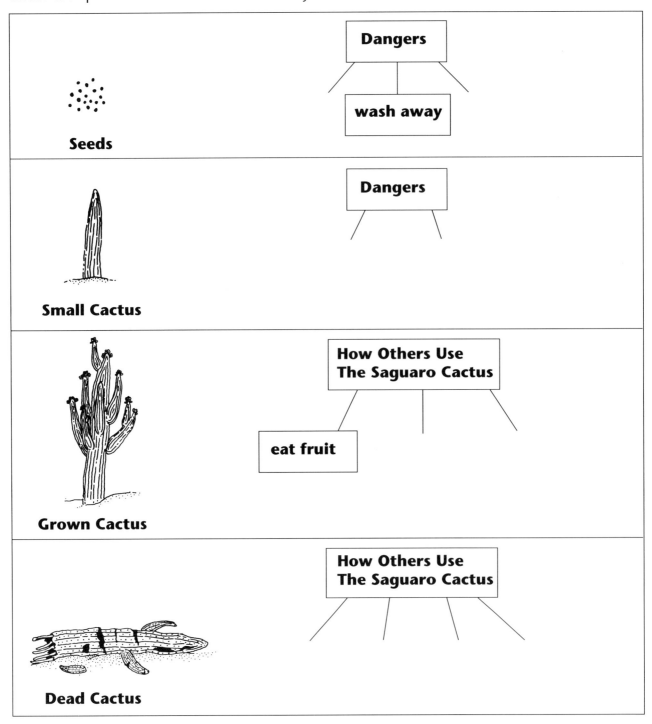

Desert Giant

Name: _____ Date: _____

LIFE CYCLE OF A SAGUARO CACTUS

Place words that describe the saguaro cactus above the pictures. Fill in key words about each topic under each picture. A few have been done for you.

Dangers

wash away

Seeds

Dangers

Small Cactus

**How Others Use
The Saguaro Cactus**

eat fruit

Grown Cactus

**How Others Use
The Saguaro Cactus**

Dead Cactus

From *Science & Stories*, published by GoodYearBooks. Copyright © 1994 Hilarie N. Staton and Tara McCarthy.

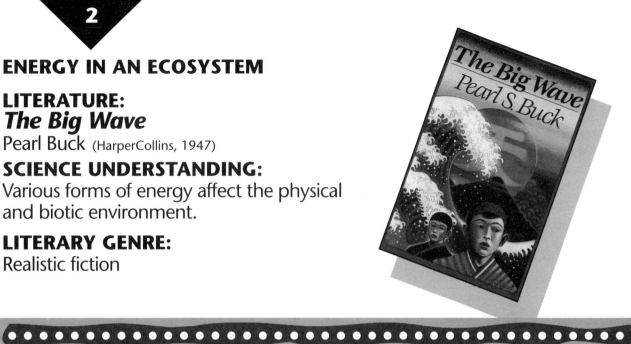

LESSON 2

ENERGY IN AN ECOSYSTEM

LITERATURE:
The Big Wave
Pearl Buck (HarperCollins, 1947)

SCIENCE UNDERSTANDING:
Various forms of energy affect the physical and biotic environment.

LITERARY GENRE:
Realistic fiction

BOOK SUMMARY

The Big Wave is a short book that clearly discusses how the people view their environment and the ways it affects their lives. Two Japanese boys, Kino and Jiya, live between a volcano and the sea. Kino's family lives on a farm on the mountainside, while Jiya lives in a village on the beach. The boys are friends, but Kino never understands why the village people hate and fear the ocean when they depend on it for their fishing. When the nearby volcano becomes very active, everyone becomes wary. As more and more things point to activity in the ocean, the Old Gentleman (a rich man on the hill) rings a warning bell to invite the villagers into his castle for protection. Jiya leaves at his family's insistence, but instead of going to the rich man's castle, he joins Kino and his father. The three watch as a wall of water scours the beach of people, boats, and houses. Jiya goes into shock and takes a long time to recover. The rich man wants to adopt him, but he forgoes being rich to live with Kino and his family on their farm. Eventually, the fishing families return, build new houses to the beach, and fish in the ocean. Jiya also returns, but brings Kino's sister with him as his wife.

PRE-READING

If you haven't used the unit introductory activity on page 46 to introduce students to survival in an ecosystem, you may want to do so now. Review the definition of an *ecosystem* (a system consisting of a living community that interacts with its physical environment).

1. Invite students to identify strong energy forces in the natural environment and the types of energy they create. Forces listed might include wind, water, lightning, earthquakes, or volcanoes, all of which can create heat energy or hydraulic (water) energy. Invite students to share experiences they have had with these forces or events they have heard about. Encourage students to think of ways people learn about these forces before they happen. (For example, scientists studying weather or volcanoes.)

2. Divide into learning groups and have each group consider one type of natural event, listing all the ways they think the event might affect people living in a nearby town. Invite each group to share their list with the class.

3. Describe the following scene to students:

> A mountain reaches down to the ocean. On its slopes, farmers grow vegetables and raise cows. Along the ocean is a small village where people fish for a living, but do not grow food because plants do not grow well in the sandy, salty soil.

Invite students to use their knowledge of ecosystems and of cultures to describe different ways the people living on the farms and those in the fishing village might interact. Encourage them to discuss trading, ideas about the sea and the soil, and helping each other in times of disaster. Display pictures of Japanese farms and fishing villages and allow students to point out things that illustrate their ideas on interdependence.

BUILDING THE SCIENCE AND LITERATURE CONNECTION

1. Distribute copies of the Study Guide. Explain that it is an organizer that they can use to organize the details from the story as they read or listen. Go over each of the questions so students understand what they are to listen or read for. After they finish the book, they will answer the last four questions.

2. Since this is a short novel, you might want to read it to students. Suggest students take notes on their Study Guides while they listen to or read the story.

3. After students have heard or read the story, divide them into small groups. Within the groups, students can share and organize the details on their Study Guide and to answer the final two questions.

4. Invite students to use their details to write two nonfiction reports about the dramatic events in *The Big Wave*. Encourage students to choose two contrasting types of writing, such as a newspaper article, a survivor's journal, a TV or radio news report, a history book passage, or a scientific report. Each report can stress a different aspect of the story's events.

5. **Evaluation.** Invite each group to share its report with the other groups. Encourage students to identify and generalize about the elements that are the same or different for different types of media.

EXTENDING THE SCIENCE
Activity 1. Students who are interested can investigate real volcanic eruptions, such as Krakatoa or Mount St. Helen's. They can locate information about the types of energy they generate and how they affect the physical and biotic environment. Encourage a group to make a volcano and/or before and after dioramas or murals to show an eruption's affect. There are also various ways to create a volcano to erupt, such as those given in *The Whole Cosmos Catalog of Science Activities* (GoodYear, 1991).

From *Science & Stories*, published by GoodYearBooks. Copyright © 1994 Hilarie N. Staton and Tara McCarthy.

Activity 2. Interested or advanced students might like to research how scientists investigate volcanoes, tsunami, hurricanes, and other violent forms of energy. Encourage students to locate information about how scientists predict these natural events, the warning systems they've developed, and the precautions they recommend. Students can present their findings in the form of interviews with experts or on bulletin boards.

Activity 3. Invite students to identify how the natural forces in Activity 2 affect people. Suggest they create a diagram showing the origin of each form of energy, forms and strength of the energy at different stages, and the affect of the energy on people. A chart for a hurricane might include the heat transfer of air and water in its creation, the wind energy transferring to trees and buildings, and the destruction created by the forceful winds and rains. More advanced students can investigate how energy is lost and what precipitates an event's end.

EXTENDING THE LITERATURE

Activity 1. Students can explore the structure of the book by creating a story map that includes the basic elements (main characters, setting, climax, problem, and solution) or other literary elements you are covering in class. Have students use some elements from the story map to create their own short stories about these characters.

Activity 2. Students might enjoy investigating how people react to and report about disasters. Play video- and audiotapes of news reports about specific disasters. Have students compare different reports and/or different media. Encourage students to share their conclusions about what makes a good report.

Activity 3. Analyze the individual characters in the book. Small groups can reread or skim the book again, so they can discuss how different characters reacted to the challenges and events in the book. They can keep a list of characteristics for each character. After the book has been analyzed, students can use their lists of characteristics to create new characters and write descriptions of how those characters would react in some crisis.

OTHER CONNECTIONS
SOCIAL STUDIES

Invite students to investigate interdependence within their own culture or within cultures they are studying in social studies. Suggest groups investigate how people depend on nature and each other. Students can create graphs or perform skits to show the relationship of people to their ecosystem and to other people who live nearby.

MATH

In *The Big Wave*, Kino's family goes on walking trips for their vacation. Suggest small groups of students create math problems about the walking trips a family could take, either in their area or in Kino's area. They can create a map or use a real one and then write problems about distance, miles walked per hour or day, projected and actual arrival times, etc. Encourage groups to edit their problems and then share them with other groups. The problems can be used as part of homework or a math center.

1. Throughout the book, the author uses many descriptions to create a picture of the land, water, and energy forces present in the environment. Students should list several details of the physical environment from these descriptions.

2. Responses should show that students grasp this general idea: while farmers and fishermen were devoted to their particular way of life, they were also aware of the ever-present threat of volcanic eruption, earthquakes, and tsunamis.

3. Answers will vary, though most students will identify or sympathize with Jiya's dilemmas: leaving and losing his family, finding a new home, and "making a career choice."

4. Answers will vary. The main energy transfer is from the heat of the earth (the volcano) to the movement of the earth to the movement of the water in the form of the tsunami.

5. Answers will vary, but include movement due to wind, water, heat, or electricity.

From *Science & Stories*, published by GoodYearBooks. Copyright © 1994 Hilarie N. Staton and Tara McCarthy.

The Big Wave

Name: _____ Date: _____

Take notes on this sheet and then share your information with your group members. Create one Study Guide with the information the group agrees on.

1. Fill in the details about the physical environment.

PHYSICAL ENVIRONMENT		
LAND	**WATER**	**ENERGY FORCES**

2. Give examples from the story of how people felt about each of the following topics.

the land:

_____

_____

the water:

_____

_____

energy forces:

_____

_____

3. Which character acted in ways similar to how you might have acted in the same circumstances? Why would you have acted that way?

_____

_____

4. Give examples from the story of how energy was transferred, transformed, or moved within the physical environment.

_____

_____

5. In what ways does energy travel within your physical environment?

_____

_____

NATURALISTS IN THE FIELD

LITERATURE:
Townsend's Warbler
Paul Fleischman (HarperCollins, 1992)

SCIENCE UNDERSTANDING:
Scientists use a variety of techniques to gather and analyze information.

LITERARY GENRE:
Biography

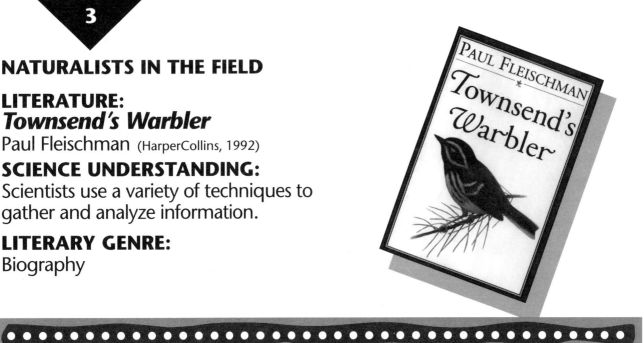

From *Science & Stories*, published by GoodYearBooks. Copyright © 1994 Hilarie N. Staton and Tara McCarthy.

BOOK SUMMARY

Townsend's Warbler tells of the trip two trained naturalists, John Kirk Townsend and Thomas Nuttall, took across North America in 1834. It contrasts this trip with that of small birds who travel from the mountains of Central America to the Pacific Northwest. Townsend and Nuttall's interests were broad, but one specialized in birds and the other in plants. During their trip to Oregon, they hoped to find (and did) many undiscovered plants and birds. The expedition the two men joined included trappers, missionaries, and men looking for land. The naturalists quickly discovered new plants and birds. They shot, dried, and gathered specimens, and also took careful notes. They traveled through buffalo herds, violent rain and hail, scorching sun, gnats, and dust storms. Through all of this, the two naturalists excitedly collected birds and flowers. They left clothes behind to make room for their specimens.

At the same time huge, flocks of small birds migrated north over Mexico and the Southwest to the Northwest's mountains. Some ventured as far as Alaska. The naturalist learned that in mid-August, the birds would return to their southern wintering grounds.

As Townsend's expedition continued into the Rockies, they encountered many adventures. When Townsend lost a journal while crossing an icy river, he had to use Nuttall's diary to reconstruct what he had written. During the last leg of the journey, a diminished party traveled through hot, waterless land. Although they came close to dehydration and starvation, the naturalists found joy in locating more specimens. Once in the Northwest, the naturalists continued to gather specimens. Then, to avoid winter, they sailed to Hawaii to explore. The explorers returned to Oregon in April so they could see the flocks of birds that would soon return from the South. It was during this exciting period that Townsend shot the small bird to be called the Townsend's warbler. First Nuttall and then Townsend returned East. They published articles about their observations and donated their specimens to museums so that all scientists could use them.

PRE-READING

If you haven't already used the unit introductory activity on page 46, you might want to do so now. Review the definition of an *ecosystem*. (a system consisting of a living community that interacts with its physical environment)

1. Have students list as many details of their ecosystems as they can recall on the chalkboard. Encourage students to categorize these details into the natural environment and manufactured parts of the environment. Using their list of natural features, invite students to identify how ancient people learned about a few of these features. Ask them how science has changed or not changed the way we learn about the natural components of the environment. Ask how people, such as the Native Americans or the early European settlers, learned how to survive in environments that were new to them.

2. Display the book jacket and ask students to predict how the Townsend's warbler got its name. Tell them that a naturalist, John Townsend, was the first scientist to record a sighting of this North American bird and so it was named for him. Invite students to predict how a naturalist living in the nineteenth century might learn about his or her environment. Encourage students to include a variety of types of observation.

3. Encourage students to play the part of a naturalist by observing their natural world and writing three journal entries for what they see. Suggest three students observe the same place, but write their journal entries without conferring. Encourage each triad to compare the details of their journal entries, the sentence structure, and descriptive phrases. Be sure students draw the conclusion that observations can be stated in a variety of acceptable ways.

BUILDING THE SCIENCE AND LITERATURE CONNECTION

1. As you read or as students read the book, *Townsend's Warbler,* have students consider the problem: How did John Townsend and Thomas Nuttall learn about the components of the ecosystems they visited? Also, suggest students use a variety of strategies to determine the meaning of words they do not know. They can use context clues, word analysis, phonics, the dictionary, or other people. You and the students can model these skills if you are reading the book aloud.

2. To do the following jigsaw cooperative learning activity, divide the class into groups of three or four students. Each member of the group rereads the book to locate details about a specific topic. One member can look for things that hindered the trip or the research of the two naturalists. The second member can identify all the ways the two naturalists learned about plants and animals. The third member can identify the details of the natural environments they passed through. If you have four members per group, this last assignment can be divided into two. One person can identify the details of the physical components of the ecosystem and the other person the details of the biotic components.

After the research has been conducted, each member shares his or her findings with the group. The group then writes at least four journal entries that Townsend and Nuttall might have written about their trip. Each journal should include details from the research of every group member.

3. After their observations are complete, encourage groups and individuals to share their journals with the class. As an **evaluation** strategy, students can create a chart of everything they have observed in their ecosystems and then write a descriptive essay about their ecosystems.

EXTENDING THE SCIENCE
Activity 1. Advanced or interested students can create classification systems of birds and plants. They can develop their own classification system for the plants and animals mentioned in the book, or choose one plant or animal and research its scientific classification.

From *Science & Stories*, published by GoodYearBooks. Copyright © 1994 Hilarie N. Staton and Tara McCarthy.

Activity 2. Students can investigate the yearly or life cycle of one type of bird. They can determine the physical needs of food, shelter, and climate of these birds, as well as where they are found, their coloration, mating, and migration patterns. After their research is complete, students can present their findings as charts, journals, stories, comic strips, or nonfiction accounts.

Activity 3. Students can compare and contrast the needs of humans and of birds within the same ecosystem. Students can investigate how each fills their basic needs (food and shelter especially) as well as the problems they have filling these needs. Students can use the following Venn Diagram to organize and present their facts.

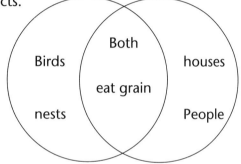

RECOMMENDED READING
Interested students can read biographies of people such as Charles Darwin, Dian Fossey, Rachel Carson, Jane Goodall, Benjamin Franklin, and John James Audubon. They can determine the processes each used to learn about ecosystems. They can create a question and answer interview to share with others.

EXTENDING THE LITERATURE
Activity 1. Students can use the factual account of an incident in the book and create a "You Are There" radio play or reader's theater play. After students have chosen their section, written any additional material, and practiced their play, they can present it to their class or another one.

Activity 2. Some students might enjoy writing journal entries about the same event from the point of view of an explorer, a naturalist, and a guide. Discuss with students what would be

important to each of these people and how that would change their views of a specific event. Students can illustrate appropriate information for each journal and display them on a bulletin board.

Activity 3. In order to share the sound of birds, students can practice and then present or record the bird poems from Paul Fleischman's book, *I Am Phoenix: Poems for Two Voices.* Invite individuals or groups to write their own two-voice poem and share them with the class.

OTHER CONNECTIONS
ART
Invite students to study several of Audubon's bird pictures, a bird watcher's sketches, and photographs of birds in nature and field guides. Encourage them to identify the different strengths and uses of each of these artistic representations. Students can compare and contrast how different people have represented the different textures of feathers. These pictures can be compared to other animal pictures to see how artists have depicted the various textures of fur, feathers, scales, and reptilian skin.

SOCIAL STUDIES/HISTORY
Explain to students that expeditions like the one Townsend and Nuttall were on would eventually change people's ideas about moving west. Encourage students to read other journals about trips along the Oregon Trail, such as Honor Morrow's *On to Oregon!* Encourage students to compare the journey these people took with the journey of a family traveling across the country today.

From *Science & Stories*, published by GoodYearBooks. Copyright © 1994 Hilarie N. Staton and Tara McCarthy.

MUSIC

Invite students to explore bird calls and songs. They can create a guessing game using purchased or self-made tapes of bird calls. Encourage pairs of students to research and analyze several bird calls. Invite each pair to teach what they've learned to at least two other pairs of students. Then divide the class into teams, placing the members of a group on different teams. Play bird calls for one team and allow them to conference to decide which bird makes that call. The opposite team can challenge them, but both teams have to identify what details in the call helped determine their choice.

Entries will vary. The chief characteristic to look for in the completed entries is the student's awareness of the variety of details within the ecosystem. Also, students need to be aware that different individuals see different details within the same ecosystem, and that together these details make up a complete picture of the ecosystem.

Townsend's Warbler

Name: _____ Date: _____

OBSERVATION GUIDE

First Observation: _____

Date: _____

Time: _____

Length of observation: _____

Location of observation: _____

Description of ecosystem as observed:

In your observation include: plants, animals, temperature, weather, manufactured items, and a sketch of something observed.

_____

_____

_____

Feelings and thoughts while observing in ecosystem.

_____

_____

Second Observation: _____

Date: _____

Time: _____

Length of observation: _____

Location of observation: _____

Description of ecosystem as observed:

In your observation include: plants, animals, temperature, weather, manufactured items, and a sketch of something observed.

_____

_____

_____

Feelings and thoughts while observing in ecosystem.

_____

_____

From *Science & Stories*, published by GoodYearBooks. Copyright © 1994 Hilarie N. Staton and Tara McCarthy.

ADAPTING TO NEW ECOSYSTEM

LITERATURE:
The Green Book
Jill Paton Walsh (Farrar, Straus, and Giroux, 1982)

SCIENCE UNDERSTANDING:
How people explore and adapt to a new ecosystem.

LITERARY GENRE:
Science fiction

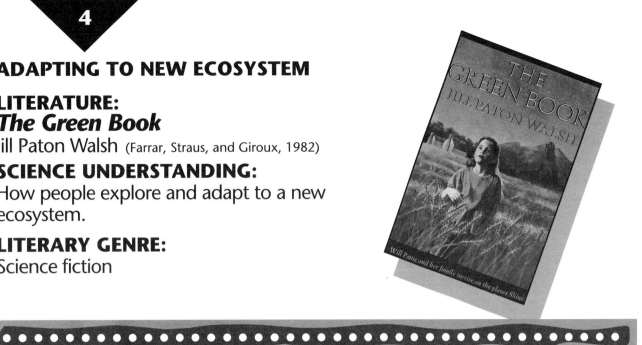

From *Science & Stories*, published by GoodYearBooks. Copyright © 1994 Hilarie N. Staton and Tara McCarthy.

BOOK SUMMARY

The earth is on the brink of disaster. Father, Pattie, Joe, and Sarah are assigned to travel to another planet in a small, old ship. They can only take a few things, including one book each. When everyone discovers Pattie's green book has blank pages, everyone laughs at her. The travelers finally land on their new planet and find it beautiful, but different. Pattie names it Shine. Trees have red leaves. There is no wind. They discover rich soil, fresh air, and water, but little animal life. They discover that the structure of the plants is different than on the earth. Some plants, like the grass, break and cut like glass. Others, like trees, are very hard. Settlers are forced to find new ways to do tasks, such as cutting down trees and building houses. Father is especially good at solving problems. He often invents and builds gadgets from his book on technology. The settlers learn to use what is in their environment to provide for their needs, such as burning jellyfish to provide light. In order to provide food, the settlers have brought animals with them, but the rabbits die after eating Shine's grass. Ever hopeful, the settlers plant the seeds they've brought, but the vegetables won't grow properly and something is wrong with the wheat. The setters begin to worry about their survival. Their hope is restored when

the children find the candy trees, whose sticky, red sap is a sweet treat.

During a picnic in a valley strewn with boulders, the children discover the boulders are moving. As they watch, giant moths emerge from the boulders. When Pattie shares candy syrup with a moth, a friendship between the two species begins. The children play and dance with the

moths until the next step in their life cycle. The moths migrate, mate, and some return to shed their wings and lay their eggs before they die.

After the moths have died, the settlers harvest the wheat. They find it has a crystalline structure, like Shine's native plants. They are afraid to eat it, but if they don't they will die. Finally, Sarah crushes some wheat, mixes it with water and makes a pancake. She and Pattie and Joe eat it. When they survive the night, the rest of the settlers decide they will try it too. Once their food shortage is solved, the settlers must develop ways to store and grind the wheat. As they get ready to survive Shine's winter, they find they can use the moths' wings for thread and cloth. The last thing they discover is that

Pattie's blank book is blank no more. In her green book, she has recorded their adventures.

PRE-READING

If you have not used the unit introductory activity on page 46 to introduce students to survival in an ecosystem, you might want to do so now. Review the definition of an *ecosystem* (a system consisting of a living community that interacts with its physical environment).

1. To introduce the genre to students, define *science fiction* (fictional stories that combine science with the author's imagination). Invite students to share examples of science fiction books, stories, movies, and television shows. Discuss how each fit the criteria of the genre and how science is integrated with imagination. Encourage students to draw the conclusion that science fiction stories, like other fiction works, include characters, action, problems, and settings.

2. Invite them to think of ways that settlers might learn about a new world. Discuss what type of problem-solving situations settlers might encounter. Invite them to predict all the ways one or two of their problems might be solved. Have groups of students write a short problem-solving situation which would be exciting and would help the settlers understand their new environment.

BUILDING THE SCIENCE AND LITERATURE CONNECTION

1. Introduce the book to students. Identify it as science fiction and encourage students to predict something about the new world from the book's cover illustration. Read the first paragraph to the students. Then, have students formulate problems that might be caused by the list Father is reading. Have them predict how these problems might affect both the book's plot and the settlers' life on their new world.

2. Pass out the Study Guide. Suggest that individuals or groups complete it while they are reading the book. If individuals are doing it, assign study groups to discuss the answers after they have completed the Study Guide. Also, discuss the answers as a class.

After students have completed and discussed the Study Guide, divide the class into small groups of three or four students. Have each group choose a different problem that confronted Shine's settlers. Once they understand their problem, encourage them to think of alternate solutions, including silly, magical, and rational ones. After they have a sizable list, have students choose one solution and rewrite the section in the book that tells how the settlers solved the problem.

Encourage the groups to share their new solutions and illustrations. Before they share their solution's summary, invite the class to tell ways that solution might change the story. Then have the group read what their summary was.

EXTENDING THE SCIENCE

Activity 1. Students can compare and contrast Shine's ecosystem and the earth's ecosystem by creating a chart of the various components of each planet. Students can also create an illustrated chart, with pictures on the earth side and their own illustrations on Shine's side. The chart can be used to write comparison paragraphs or essays.

Activity 2. Interested or advanced students can investigate the structure of different types of plants and minerals and build models of the molecules or cross-sections of the matter to show how different substances cut and break in different ways. They can create displays to share with other students.

From *Science & Stories*, published by GoodYearBooks. Copyright © 1994 Hilarie N. Staton and Tara McCarthy.

EXTENDING THE LITERATURE

Activity 1. Students can explore problems in our ecosystem that science is trying to solve. They can identify these problems by skimming newspapers or watching television news programs. Students can then research the problems. Encourage students to create a file or bulletin board of their findings. Then groups or individuals can identify ways they might help. Invite individual students to write a letter to their classmates or to the local newspaper detailing their ideas about the problem and their possible solutions.

Activity 2. Student might conduct a survey, asking people what books they'd take with them on a space voyage.

RECOMMENDED READING

Students might like to compare the Shine ecosystem with the ecosystem described in Lawrence Yep's *Sweetwater.* They can also find poems about the earth, and use one of them as a model to write a poem about Shine.

OTHER CONNECTIONS
HISTORY

Invite students to create a pictorial comparison chart to show how local Native Americans, European settlers, and Shine's settlers solved similar problems. Problems might include finding food, creating shelter, using plants both for cooking (herbs) and for medicine, and using the natural environment. Encourage students to share their findings with their classmates or with other classes who are studying local history.

ART

Encourage students to investigate science fiction art that depicts imaginary places. The covers of science fiction novels, especially paperback books, are one source of these imaginative and detailed pictures. Then have students create illustrations or sculptures based on passages from *The Green Book.* Display these works of art in the library to encourage others to read this novel.

MATH

Have students choose partners. Invite each pair to choose a topic from the book to use as the basis for math word problems. For instance, one group might write about the trip from the earth, another about the population's future growth or the moth people of Shine. Suggest that students invent the necessary numbers, but remain true to the story and characters. Encourage a variety of problems, such as problems about time, distance, and quantity, as well as both simple and more complex problems. After the problems are written, have student pairs trade problems.

STUDY GUIDE TIPS

Through discussion, groups and partners will come up with answers that satisfy them. However, since the answers may vary from team to team, remind students to note the book pages after their answers for easy reference as the class shares and compares responses.

The Green Book

Name: _____ Date: _____

Make notes on this page as you read. Then use separate pieces of paper to summarize what you have learned.

Chapter 1

1. As you read the chapter, list the things you find that might have an important effect on life on the settler's new planet. These might be items or events.

_____

_____

2. What are some possible problems that the settlers might have at their new home?

_____

_____

Chapter 2

3. As you read the chapter, list details of the new environment. For each one, predict either a problem that it will cause or how it will help settlers solve a basic problem, such as finding food.

New environment	Predicted problem or solution

Chapters 3 and 4

4. What are some of the ways Shine's settlers are meeting their basic needs for food, shelter, and fuel?

_____

_____

Which are components of Shine's ecosystem?

_____

_____

5. List two problems Shine's settlers haven't solved yet and two possible solutions for each.

_____

_____

From *Science & Stories*, published by GoodYearBooks. Copyright © 1994 Hilarie N. Staton and Tara McCarthy.

Chapters 5 and 6

6. As you read the chapter, list the details of the moth people's life.

   _____

   _____

7. After you have finished the chapter, create a hypothetical life cycle of the moth people based on the facts from the book.

   _____

   _____

8. What are some ways the settlers might use or share their world with the moth people?

   _____

   _____

Chapter 7

After you have finished the book, answer the following questions:

9. In what ways did the settlers adapt to Shine's ecosystem to solve their problems? Which of these ways involved the use of technology?

   _____

   _____

10. What components of Shine's ecosystem did the settlers use to solve their problems and how did this change Shine's ecosystem?

    _____

    _____

11. If you wrote *The Green Book,* would you have solved the problems the same way as the author did? Give examples and tell what you think of the author's solution.

    _____

    _____

12. How can you apply what you learned about the settlers and Shine's ecosystem to how we live on the earth?

    _____

    _____

INTERACTIONS AFFECTING AN ECOSYSTEM

LITERATURE:
Julie of the Wolves
Jean Craighead George (HarperCollins, 1974)

SCIENCE UNDERSTANDING:
Changes in one part of an ecosystem (such as animal populations, weather, seasons, or human interaction) affect life in other parts of the ecosystem.

LITERARY GENRE:
Realistic fiction

BOOK SUMMARY

Julie, or Miyax, leaves her young husband and civilization to walk across the Arctic tundra to the sea and the modern world of her San Francisco pen pal. She is close to starvation when she encounters a pack of wolves. She observes them carefully, learns their nonverbal language, copies it, and eventually is accepted as a member of the pack. Her survival depends on her remembering her father's lessons of the old ways as well as the protection of the wolf leader, Amaroq. She survives the summer and short fall by being accepted as a wolf pup, sharing their food, hunting various vegetation and small animals, cooking over a fire of dried caribou droppings, and watching the birds. Along with her pack, she begins the trip toward the coast and civilization. When she is closer to the ocean, a hunter kills the leader of the pack and wounds the young male who has grown up with Miyax that summer. Miyax nurses this young wolf back to health, but this episode helps her decide that her dream of moving to San Francisco is a false one. She'd rather remain a traditional Eskimo. An Eskimo couple stop on their way to hunt caribou. They tell Miyax of

the wise hunter from their village. His name and teachings are the same as her presumed dead father, so she goes to investigate. Her disappointment in what she finds helps her decide what her future will be.

PRE-READING

If you haven't used the unit introductory activity on page 46, use it now to have students review the definition of an *ecosystem* (a system consisting of a living community that interacts with its physical environment) and survival in an ecosystem.

1. To introduce the book to students, hold up the book and invite students to examine the cover and illustrations. Encourage them to predict the type of ecosystem they will be reading about (the Arctic tundra). Have the class think of all the phrases and words an author might use to describe the Arctic. Write this class list on paper, so students can add to and edit it as you read the book.

2. Invite small groups of students to write or illustrate action scenes that show what a person might need to do to survive in the

Arctic and to share these scenes with the rest of the class. As they watch the scenes, encourage students to predict specific effects these events might have on other components of the ecosystem. For example, hunting might mean fewer animals.

3. Hold up a picture of an Arctic wolf. With the class, make three lists:

   • what students know about wolves;
   • what students think they know, but are not sure is really true; and
   • questions they want answered about wolves.

BUILDING THE SCIENCE AND LITERATURE CONNECTION

1. Before students begin reading this book, write the following questions where they can remain throughout the lesson. Suggest students consider these two problems as they read, listen and work in groups:

   • How do changes in one area of an ecosystem affect other areas of the ecosystem?
   • How do authors use descriptions, events, and dialog to describe the physical and living parts of an ecosystem and the relationships between these parts?

2. Assign, or have students choose, cooperative learning groups of 3-4 students. Distribute the Arctic Study Guide and assign each group a different topic listed below. If you have a large class or students are working in pairs, more than one group can work on the same topic.

Topics:
   • Weather (including temperature and fog)
   • Small animals (including lemmings and birds)
   • Plants (including grasses, moss, and lichens)
   • Seasons (including day and night)
   • Land and water forms
   • Human technology
   • Large animals (including caribou and bears)
   • Wolves

Be sure all group members write their topics in all of the blanks on their Study Guides. Explain that by answering specific questions about their topic, they will find it easier to answer the major questions at the end. Encourage groups to work together to answer the Study Guide questions. Their answers don't need to be identical, but the group should agree that each one's answers are correct. For example, each group member might choose different examples to support their conclusions. Explain that each group will create a project to share their findings with the class.

3. Read the book to the class, or have each student read it. While they are reading the book, have the groups meet at regular intervals—at least after each part—to discuss the Study Guide questions and their topic. Encourage students to use outside reference sources to add to their knowledge of their topic.

4. **Evaluation.** After students have completed the reading, have each group create their visual, written, or dramatic presentation about their topic. Encourage each group to share their presentation with the class. Invite all students to discuss how each topic fits into the general Arctic ecosystem. Students can also compare components and relationships in their own ecosystem. Encourage students to make generalizations about the questions introduced before they began the book.

EXTENDING THE SCIENCE
Activity 1. Students can research the yearly cycles or life cycles of such Arctic animals as grizzly bears, lemmings, caribou, or wolves and create charts, murals, dances, or stories based on their findings.

From *Science & Stories*, published by GoodYearBooks. Copyright © 1994 Hilarie N. Staton and Tara McCarthy.

Activity 2. Interested or advanced students might like to create classification charts of Arctic plants and animals. More advanced students can establish many criteria for their classifications, while less advanced students might only use a very obvious two or three characteristics. Students can share their classification system with the class.

Activity 3. Some students can explore time as it relates to days and nights or light and dark in the Arctic region. A graph or chart can be developed to show the changing light levels and how people cope with them.

Activity 4. Interested students might like to investigate wolves and then rearrange and add information to the Know You Know/Think You Know/Want to Know chart created during the Pre-reading activity. Students can also do further research on such topics as wolves' nonverbal communication and social structure. Suggest they use books, such as Jean Craighead George's *The Moon of the Gray Wolves.* Invite students to share their findings.

EXTENDING THE LITERATURE
Activity 1. Interested students can review and add to their list of descriptions of the Arctic ecosystem (from the Pre-reading activity). They can use these lists to write descriptive poems about the Arctic. Able students can include action scenes that also help define the Arctic ecosystem within the poetic format.

Activity 2. Some students can investigate the structure of *Julie of the Wolves,* which includes flashbacks that can be confusing to some students. Other students can create a timeline of Julie's life by placing events on 3" by 5" cards and arranging them in chronological order rather than the order they are discussed in the book. Advanced students can analyze the various devices the author used and write a story using one of them.

Activity 3. Learning groups can each identify one important problem from the book, how it is

resolved, an alternative resolution, and how that alternative resolution would have changed the events in the story.

OTHER CONNECTIONS
GEOGRAPHY/MATH
If students are unfamiliar with how to use a map's scale, introduce the concept using a local map. Then present an Alaska state map for students to examine. Compare the scale and some distances on each map. Help students draw the conclusion that Alaska has vast distances. Invite students to write math word problems using the Alaska map, local map, or both. They can ask distance questions, total mileage questions, or comparison questions, depending on their level of expertise. Each student can solve another student's problems and offer editing suggestions about the clarity and accuracy of the problems. Collect the edited problems and, if necessary, re-edit them. Use them as part of a classwork or homework assignment.

SOCIAL STUDIES
Invite students to investigate traditional Eskimo or Inuit culture. Have them create charts like the following one to show how these people meet their basic needs. Besides the topics suggested, students might investigate topics such as water use, clothes, holidays, and religion. Students can take notes on their chart/organizer and then fill in the same information about their own cultures. Have students compare and contrast the two cultures.

From *Science & Stories*, published by GoodYearBooks. Copyright © 1994 Hilarie N. Staton and Tara McCarthy.

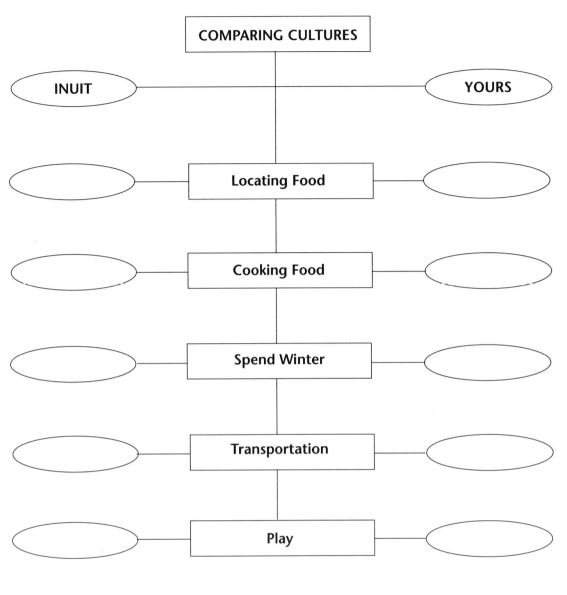

COMPARING CULTURES

INUIT — YOURS

Locating Food

Cooking Food

Spend Winter

Transportation

Play

STUDY GUIDE TIPS

1. Parts I, II, and III. Ask groups to write page references indicating where they found their information or got their ideas.
2. Final questions: Use the responses from 1-5 as the basis for a class discussion.

Julie of the Wolves

Name:_____ Date:_____

Problem: How do(es) _____ interact with and affect the Arctic's physical environment, plants, and animals?

Write your topic in the problem above and in the blanks in the Study Guide questions. Answer these questions about *Julie of the Wolves* as you read the book.

Part I

1. How does Julie learn about the Arctic and how to survive in it?

_____

_____

2. Copy a description from the book that makes the Arctic ecosystem seem real and vivid to you. This description might include actions and dialog.

_____

_____

3. Describe two important elements of the Arctic ecosystem that are different from your ecosystem.

_____

_____

4. How do Julie and the wolves interact with _____? Describe how the interaction affects them and other parts of the Arctic ecosystem.

_____

_____

5. How has Miyax adapted to the Arctic ecosystem by the end of Part I?

_____

_____

Part II

1. Copy a description or summarize an event in the book that makes Arctic village life seem real and vivid to you.

_____

_____

2. Describe some ways the people in the Arctic have adapted to their ecosystem.

_____

_____

From *Science & Stories*, published by GoodYearBooks. Copyright © 1994 Hilarie N. Staton and Tara McCarthy.

3. Does _____ have the same relationship to the village's survival as it did to Julie's survival in Part I? Explain why or why not.

_____

_____

Part III

1. Identify how parts of the Arctic ecosystem are influenced by the changes in _____ that have happened since the beginning of the book.

_____

_____

2. What parts of the ecosystem are responsible for the changes Miyax encounters on her walk west?

_____

_____

Final Questions

1. Choose the four parts of the Arctic ecosystem that you think were the most important to Julie's survival. Explain why you chose each.

_____

_____

2. Do you think Jean Craighead George's descriptions were scientifically accurate? Give examples to support your opinion. Your examples can be from this book and other sources too.

_____

_____

3. Based on this book, write a statement about how humans can affect an ecosystem. Write another statement about how ecosystems can affect humans.

_____

_____

4. Write four ways that you have affected an ecosystem. Be specific.

_____

_____

5. What was the most important thing you learned about ecosystems as you read this book? How will you use this new knowledge?

_____

_____

Plan a presentation to show your classmates how _____ interacts with and affects the Arctic's physical environment, plants, and animals.

_____

_____

TECHNOLOGY

SCIENCE UNDERSTANDINGS

In this unit, students explore technology and its relationship to science and society. Students develop the following understandings.

1. Technology is often developed in response to problems in society.

2. Technology applies scientific principles and concepts to do work easier and faster.

3. Technology often changes the environment or daily life.

4. Energy takes various forms and often changes within a complex system.

UNIT MAP

Each lesson revolves around one or more pieces of children's literature, emphasizes a literary genre or strategy, and focuses on a problem students can solve as they work through the lesson.

Lesson	Literature	Genre/Strategy	Problem
1	**Machines and How They Work**	Nonfiction	How do machines use scientific principles and concepts to do work?
2	**Dragonwings**	Realistic fiction	What methods do people use as they develop a new technology?
3	**The Twenty-one Balloons**	Fantasy	Which scientific principles and concepts are the basis for specific technological devices?
4	**City: A Story of Roman Planning and Construction**	History	How can technology solve problems that are part of daily life?
5	**Lyddie**	Historical fiction	How can technological changes affect society?

From *Science & Stories*, published by GoodYearBooks. Copyright © 1994 Hilarie N. Staton and Tara McCarthy.

INTRODUCING THE TECHNOLOGY UNIT

1. Invite students to give various examples of technology. Encourage them to include machines, medical advances, and products. Make a permanent class list that students can add to and refer to during the unit. If students are having trouble coming up with suggestions, suggest they develop a list of non technology items and processes of natural origin. After they have developed these two lists, work with them to create a definition of *technology*. Although there are at least four definitions, the two they need to be aware of are:

   - non-natural objects of all kinds manufactured by people (This is the most common definition.)
   - a system or process in which tools and/or machines and human power work together to increase people's ability to do tasks and thus change their environment

2. Divide the class into small groups. Invite each group to choose one example of recent technology in their daily life, such as video-recorders, microwave ovens, or video games. Pass out the interview sheet and go over the questions with students. Encourage them to suggest other questions they might want to ask about their specific technological device. To ensure a cross-section of experiences, have each student in the group interview a different person, including those of different ages and experiences.

3. After each student has completed his or her interview, have the group compile its findings onto a chart. Draw conclusions about how people feel about each technology, how people use it, whether it has changed their lives, whether it has created problems, and whether it is worthwhile. In a class discussion, invite each group to share their findings and conclusions. Work with the class to create a hypothesis about how science and society are influenced by technology and technological changes, and how technology is influenced by what people think.

INTRODUCING THE SYNTHESIS ACTIVITY

1. If you are planning to use the Final Unit Synthesis Activity, tell students they will be reading books that relate to technology. As they read, they should think about the relationships between science, technology and people, both today and in the past. Warn students that at the unit's end they will be creating their own imaginary technology and will have to analyze it for scientific principles and to predict its effect on people.

2. Suggest students keep all their technology activities together in a portfolio so that they can review the various relationships they discover before they begin their final project. This portfolio can also be used for assessment purposes.

CARRYING OUT THE UNIT SYNTHESIS ACTIVITY

This activity allows students to use what they have learned about the relationships of science, technology, and society in your science and social studies programs and from the literature. This project can be used to assess the students' knowledge of the basic concepts about these relationships.

> **Objective:** To develop some type of technology, analyze the scientific principles it uses and predict the ways it will impact society.

Step 1. Create several cooperative learning groups and challenge each group to develop an imaginary form of technology that might change the world. Groups should consider the following questions:

- What does your technology do?
- Will it help people do more than one thing?
- What problem does this technology solve for people?
- Describe your technology and exactly how people use it.

- What scientific principles, concepts, or ideas does it use? Include the type of energy necessary to use it.
- If this technology became very popular, how might it change people's lives?
- Predict problems your technology might create.

Step 2. After students have analyzed their technologies, they can create graphics that explain them and the scientific principles behind them.

Step 3. Students can then write stories about how or why each technology was invented (in response to what problem), or about this technology in the future (how it is used, who benefits from it, the changes it creates, the problems it creates). Emphasize these are fictional stories, but are based on how technology can cause changes in society and how society can cause new technology to develop.

Step 4. Invite each group to share their technology with the class. Encourage classmates to question each group about how this new technology will affect them.

INTEGRATION ACTIVITIES
The connection activities can be done while the students are reading the books or after they have completed it. These activities connect the general unit theme to other content areas in especially creative ways.

POETRY CONNECTION
Share some poetry about technology with the class, such as Carl Sandburg's Chicago poems. Invite students to use scientific and technological terms, as well as figurative and descriptive language, to write a poem about one specific type of technology. Encourage them to take a consistent attitude toward their topic through their choice of words, phrases, and details.

HISTORY CONNECTION
Invite small groups of students to investigate eras of major technological change. By investigating the times and places they are studying in social studies, they can relate how people react to and are affected by these changes. The students might investigate what happened when migrant cultures developed agriculture, when a culture learned to use wheeled vehicles, or when electricity became available to industry and homes. Students can also interview adults about how computers and electronics have changed their lives.

ART CONNECTION
Invite students to create pictures of past, present, or future scenes that include technology. Encourage them to show a specific point of view through their use of color, details, and action. They can create realistic or impressionistic pictures or collages. One picture might show people cheerfully riding around in the country in a car, while another might show many cars spewing out smog as they travel concrete highways.

MATH CONNECTION
Encourage small groups of students to visualize a task, such as traveling between two places or toasting a piece of bread, before and after the introduction of a specific technology. Students can create fact charts comparing the speeds at which the task was done before and after the technology. They can write a series of word problems that require the information on the chart. These word problems can be used in a math center, as homework, or as review assignments.

ADDITIONAL MATERIALS YOU MIGHT WANT TO USE
For additional materials you might want to use with this unit, see Additional Resources, pages 130-134.

From *Science & Stories*, published by GoodYearBooks. Copyright © 1994 Hilarie N. Staton and Tara McCarthy.

Name: _____ Date: _____

INTERVIEW SHEET

TECHNOLOGY:

Ask someone these questions about the technology your group has chosen. Write your answers and then share them with your group.

1. How did you learn about this new technology?

_____

_____

2. Did you do this task before you had this technology? If yes, ask the following questions:

   • How did you do it before?

   _____

   • Do you like using the new process better than the old?_____

   _____

   • Which is easier, the new way or the old way? Give some examples.

   _____

   • Did you use the old method very often? _____

   • Do you use the new method more often than you used to use the old? _____

3. What positive changes has the new technology created in your life?

_____

_____

4. Has the new technology created any problems for you or others? What are they?

_____

_____

5. How have you solved these problems?

_____

_____

6. Is this technology worth having around? Why do you think as you do?

_____

_____

7. What changes would you make to this technology to make it better or easier to use?

_____

_____

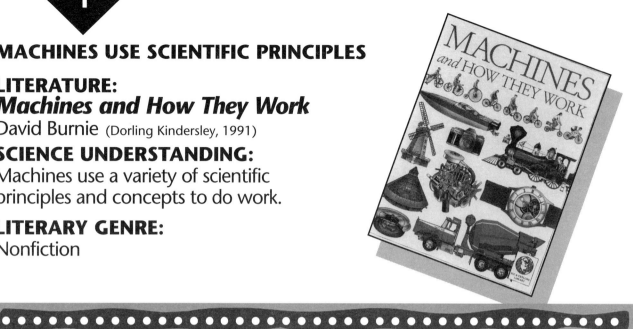

LESSON 1

MACHINES USE SCIENTIFIC PRINCIPLES

LITERATURE:
Machines and How They Work
David Burnie (Dorling Kindersley, 1991)

SCIENCE UNDERSTANDING:
Machines use a variety of scientific principles and concepts to do work.

LITERARY GENRE:
Nonfiction

BOOK SUMMARY

Machines and How They Work begins by defining machines and then discusses early machines, both simple and more complex ones. The clear illustrations show each device at work. Each large, double page spread is well illustrated with a minimum amount of clearly written text about machines that do a variety of tasks. Most have at least one machine in a cutaway view that is labeled. Some pictures, like those under "time and motion" and "bicycles," show the development of the modern machine. Sundials, wrist watches, water wheels, modern hydro-electric generators, sewing machines, and cars are clearly illustrated. Unusual and intriguing machines, such as the hovercraft, jackhammers, and cranes, are also included. A few processes, such as drilling for oil in the ocean, are discussed in more detail than others. The text is not low vocabulary but is clearly written and, along with the clear illustrations, can be understood fairly easily. This is part of Dorling Kindersley's excellent "See and Explore Library."

PRE-READING

You might want to introduce technology with the unit introductory activity on page 75, if you haven't already.

1. Invite students to identify all the examples of machines on the list they developed during that introductory activity. As they identify and discuss the characteristics common to these machines, help them create a list of characteristics all machines share. List these on the chalkboard. Read to students the first paragraph on page 4 in *Machines and How They Work*. Discuss the book's definition of machines and other definitions students might have encountered in science.

2. After you read the second paragraph on page 4, discuss machines and energy sources with students. Tie the book's information with science concepts they already know. Review important terms and concepts such as *force* (a push or pull on an object that causes it to move) and *energy* (the ability to do work). Review *simple machines* in their various forms (levers, including the wheel and axle; fixed and moveable pulleys, including drive belts; and inclined planes, including wedges and screws); and *complex machines* (machines that are made up of more than one simple machine). You might want to review simple machines by having students perform a series of activities, such as moving a brick with pulleys, inclined planes,

and levers. Small groups can try various simple machines and share their results with the class.

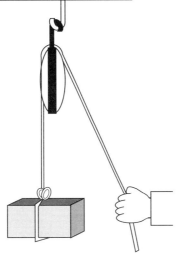

3. Invite students to think about what machines people living in earlier times might have used. Then have students read, examine, and discuss pages 6 and 7 and then 8 and 9 in the book, *Machines*. Have students identify and discuss each simple machine listed. Encourage them to examine the energy sources, how energy is transferred within the system, what work is actually being done, and how they think this machine changed life for the people who lived when it was invented.

4. Divide the class into small groups and have each group write a short, clear description of one of the machines on pages 6 through 9. Encourage each group to write a few figurative phrases about its machine.

BUILDING THE SCIENCE AND LITERATURE CONNECTION

You can read the entire book *Machines* to the class or use it as a reference and starting point for the following activity.

1. Create cooperative learning groups of four to six students. Invite each group to choose one machine from the book *Machines* or any other machine about which they can locate enough information.

2. Pass out the Study Guide and discuss it with students. On it, each group answers five basic questions about its machine. Then each group member writes a short poem about a different aspect of the machine.

3. Finally, each member completes one of the following activities or one of their own involving their machine. Encourage group members to act as reference sources, editors, and cheerleaders for each other. The variety of activities listed below allows students to choose one that uses their strengths and interests. There are many other possible ones.

- Make a detailed, labeled diagram of the machine or a cross-section of it.
- Investigate life before and after the advent of this machine. Write several scenes or do a series of illustrations to show how the machine has changed, modified, or influenced daily life.
- Make a timeline to show the development from simple tools to this more complex machine. Include possible future machines that might develop from it.
- Research and report on a person important in the development of this machine. This could be an inventor, manufacturer, or business person involved with its production or sale.
- Investigate and report on the scientific principles and concepts by which this machine operates.

4. **Evaluation.** You might want to give each member of the class a comment sheet that they can use to evaluate the other groups' presentation. This might include questions or scales such as the following:

- How well did the group research and present the various aspects of the machine?
- How well did their explanations or illustrations show the important science principles? Did all parts of the presentation relate to the machine?
- Did the group make an interesting, informative, and well-rehearsed presentation?

EXTENDING THE SCIENCE

Activity 1. Interested or advanced students might want to investigate machines with various energy sources, such as wind, water, electric, or solar power. Students can create charts or diagrams to show how energy is moved through the system and where and when it changes form.

Activity 2. Students might like to build their own complex machines using a variety of simple machines. These can be drawn on paper or constructed out of found materials, such as broken toys, machines, and polystryene packing. Encourage students to display their machines and their purposes in a technology fair.

Activity 3. Artistic students might enjoy creating a cutaway view of a complex machine, and labelling the simple machines and scientific principles that make up that machine. The drawings can be posted around the room.

EXTENDING THE LITERATURE

Activity 1. Students might want to write a letter to an imaginary pen pal who has never seen a common machine. They might write to a pal in South America who has never seen a toaster or blender. In the letter they can clearly describe the machine, its use, and its place in their life. Invite them to use illustrations, clear descriptions, and figurative language in their letters. Encourage them to share their letters with each other.

Activity 2. Students can write stories that tell how someone depends upon one machine for a specific reason. The plots can involve the consequences when the machine is lost, its source of energy fails, or the character can not reach it in time. Combine these stories in a book of machine fiction or with stories from other technology lessons.

Activity 3. Students who enjoy a challenge might enjoy writing a poem or story from the viewpoint of the machine. They can write riddle poems or poems that use descriptive and figurative language to describe the machine or task it does.

Activity 4. Students can add a new chapter to the book *Machines* about machines that are not covered in it. They can research, write, and illustrate their own versions using clear, detailed text and labeled illustrations. Bind the new chapters together to create a *More Machines and How They Work* book.

OTHER CONNECTIONS
ART
Students can create collages of various models of a general category of machines (i.e., transportation machines) or of a specific type of machine (i.e., cars). Within the collage both similarities and differences can be emphasized. Have students speak about these similarities and differences as they share their collages with their classmates.

MUSIC
Introduce student to music based on mechanical sounds or that uses machines, such as Tchaikovsky's *1812 Overture,* which uses cannons. Encourage students to suggest their own additions to musical pieces you present. You might play and describe segments from operas (*Copeila* by Delibes, which is about the construction of a mechanical doll), from celebrator pieces (the *1812 Overture*), or from movie music that captures the feeling of technology (*Star Wars*).

DANCE
Invite students to create a dance based on a machine or on mechanical actions. Individuals can mimic simple machines, or a group can work together to imitate a complex machine. Students can invent or imitate actions. Encourage students to locate or write music as background for their dances and to write narratives to go along with the movements. Encourage groups and individuals to perform their dance for the class or a wider audience.

From *Science & Stories,* published by GoodYearBooks. Copyright © 1994 Hilarie N. Staton and Tara McCarthy.

SOCIAL STUDIES

Create a class timeline of machines. Using the information in *Machines* and other books, have each student locate or draw a picture of one machine and research when it was invented or first used. You may want to assign specific machines so that the timeline includes simple, early machines as well as modern, complex ones.

STUDY GUIDE TIPS

Students answers will vary depending on the machine and sources chosen. Remind students to list the titles of any sources they use to find information about their machine.

Machines and How They Work

Name: _____ Date: _____

I. As a group, read *Machines and How They Work.* With your group, choose one machine described after page 9. Use the information in the book and from other sources to answer the following questions about your machine.

1. Identify the simple machines that are part of the complex machine.

_____

_____

_____

2. What type of energy does your machine use?

_____

_____

_____

3. How is the energy transferred or changed as it travels through the machine?

_____

_____

_____

4. What work is done by the machine?

_____

_____

_____

5. How does the machine affect people's lives?

_____

_____

_____

II. Your teacher will suggest some projects. Each member of your group chooses a different project involving your machine. Help other group members by suggesting sources, sharing information, and editing their activities. Share with the class all the poems and projects that your group has created.

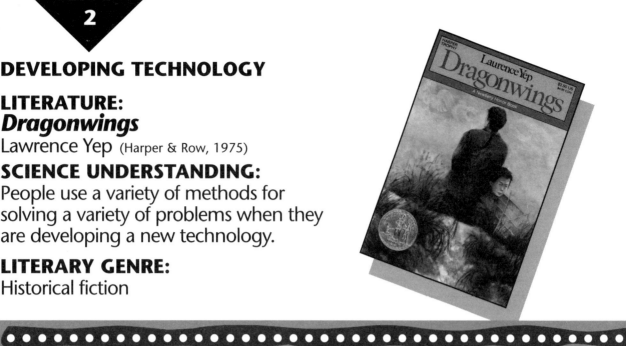

DEVELOPING TECHNOLOGY

LITERATURE:
Dragonwings
Lawrence Yep (Harper & Row, 1975)

SCIENCE UNDERSTANDING:
People use a variety of methods for solving a variety of problems when they are developing a new technology.

LITERARY GENRE:
Historical fiction

BOOK SUMMARY

Dragonwings is the story of how Windrider, a Chinese immigrant, follows and fulfills his dream to build an aeroplane. His young son, Moon Shadow, travels from China to join him in San Francisco, where they live and work in the family's laundry. The very hard and harrowing life of the Chinese in 1903 America becomes real through the adventures of Moon Shadow, his father, uncles, and cousins. These experiences include opium dens, family feuds, organized crime, prejudice, and racial violence. They also include love and support and, always, Windrider's dream of having been a powerful dragon in another life. Windrider likes to build technological devices like crystal sets (an early radio) and is a master kitemaker. But he really wants to learn as much as he can about flying machines so he can build one.

Windrider and Moon Shadow take a bold step and move outside Chinatown, into the world of the "demons." Moon Shadow takes care of his father's house and becomes friends with their landlady, Miss Whitlaw, and her niece, Robin. Moon Shadow teaches them about his world and they teach him about their world. During this time, Moon Shadow surprises his father by beginning a correspondence with the Wright Brothers. This correspondence becomes an important source of information for Windrider. He further refines his kites and aeroplane models.

When the San Francisco earthquake of 1906 hits, many people draw together to help each other, while others can not overcome their prejudices. By helping both Miss Whitlaw and their family, Windrider and Moon Shadow draw the two diverse groups of people together for a moment. Eventually Windrider and Moon Shadow move to a huge, drafty barn in Oakland. They work, but spend all their money on the airplane models and the airplane that Windrider has designed. Finally, about to be dispossessed because they can't pay the rent, the father and son are close to giving up. However, their friends and family come through for them, surprising them with funds, physical labor, and emotional support. On that day Windrider flies. After he crashes, he decides to change the focus of his life and bring his beloved wife over to America from China. He has reached one dream and will now reach for another.

PRE-READING

If you have not done the unit introductory activity on page 75 to introduce students to technology, you might want to do it now.

1. Afterwards, invite students to identify various thinking processes a scientist or engineer might use as he or she develops new technology. Students might suggest questioning, experimenting, and researching. Encourage students to list the personal traits these people might have or need to be successful. These might include being dedicated, observant, and careful.

2. Introduce the book *Dragonwings* to students by telling them that the author got the idea for the story when he read an old newspaper article about a young Chinese flier in Oakland, California (see Afterword in the book). Although the story and characters are fictional, the general setting (early 1900s San Francisco) is real. Ask students to pretend they are Lawrence Yep, as he is planning to write this book. Encourage them to identify all the traits they believe this flier will need in order to succeed.

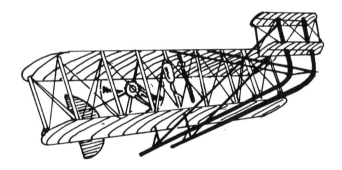

BUILDING THE SCIENCE AND LITERATURE CONNECTION

1. Before you pass out the Study Guide, divide the class into study groups. Each group will be responsible for completing and turning in one Study Guide, but all students should take note on the Study Guide questions as they read the chapter. All group members should contribute to the Study Guide discussions. You might want to provide specific roles to group members (recorder, question reader, fact locator, etc.). As you read the book aloud or as individual students read it to themselves, have the groups meet to discuss

each chapter and add details to their study guide chart.

2. **Evaluation.** Invite each group to create a project that shows the problems that got in the way of Windrider fulfilling his dream and the personal traits that helped him overcome them. Students might also create timelines with pictures, comic books or strips, news broadcasts, or murals. Encourage students to present their projects to the class.

EXTENDING THE SCIENCE

Activity 1. Interested students might want to experiment with aerodynamics by building paper airplanes, with a variety of shapes to the wings, tails, and bodies. Have students test their airplanes, record their results, and then evaluate the results for specific factors that are important in getting the paper planes (or any plane) to fly. Students should create scientific reports that give the results of their experiments, so others can duplicate their efforts.

Activity 2. Students interested in old planes can investigate how the Wright Brothers developed and improved their airplanes. Students can write interviews, biographical sketches, or visual presentations to compare the Wright Brothers' experiences with those of Windrider.

Activity 3. Interested or advanced students can identify and give examples of some of the scientific principles and concepts Windrider needed to know before he could create his kites, plane models, and airplane. Students can do a poster illustrating each concept and display them around the room.

Activity 4. Interested students can investigate what is necessary to make a successful kite and then create their own kites in a variety of shapes and sizes. Invite those who are willing to do a demonstration flight for the class.

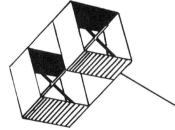

From *Science & Stories*, published by GoodYearBooks. Copyright © 1994 Hilarie N. Staton and Tara McCarthy.

EXTENDING THE LITERATURE

Activity 1. Interested students might want to write an interview or newspaper article about Windrider and Moon Shadow that centers on the problems they faced in getting Dragonwings to fly. These can be gathered together into a magazine and shared with the class.

Activity 2. Students interested in science can create Windrider's scientific journal. This might include information about his research, his feelings, his experiments, and his results. These can be compared to a real scientist's journal or with what other students have written.

RECOMMENDED READING

Interested students might enjoy researching and retelling a variety of dragon stories from different cultures. These can be gathered and illustrated for a book or used for storytelling to younger students.

OTHER CONNECTIONS
ART

Invite a person who writes Chinese characters to demonstrate this art to the class. Suggest that your speaker discuss the representational aspect of the characters with students as well as show them how to create a few. Encourage students to draw characters using ink and brush in order to send each other messages, or as part of greeting cards that send such wishes as "good luck" or "Happy New Year."

MATH

Windrider tells Moon Shadow about the ratios necessary to create a model. Invite small groups of students to use a model airplane, car, ship, or space vehicle to determine the size of the original. Ratios are usually given on the model box or instructions. Students can measure the plastic pieces and then use the ratio to figure out the original size. They can create a chart with their findings and share it with the class or write math problems using the chart.

SOCIAL STUDIES

Invite students to use the book to identify some of the problems faced by of the Chinese who came to the American West in the late 1800s and early 1900s. Encourage students to locate more information about their lives. Then have students compare their problems with those faced by the immigrants who settle their own area. Encourage students to draw conclusions about the general problems faced by many ethnic groups, and those that were unique to the Chinese.

STUDY GUIDE TIPS

Because answers will vary, you may wish to bring the class together after groups complete the answers for each chapter so they can share their responses before they go on to the next chapter. This is a useful strategy for both reviewing and pre-viewing, for making sure students with reading problems have gotten the main points, and for enriching all students' understanding as they move along in the story.

From *Science & Stories*, published by GoodYearBooks. Copyright © 1994 Hilarie N. Staton and Tara McCarthy.

Dragonwings

Name:_____ Date:_____

After you read each chapter of *Dragonwings,* think about Windrider and the goal he wants to reach: building and flying an airplane.

Write down the ways he goes about reaching his dream and the problems that interfere with his reaching it. Notice how other people, communication, personality, feelings, and research play a part in his life.

	How did Windrider work toward his dream?	What problems interfered with Windrider reaching his dream?
Chapters 1-3		
Chapter 4		
Chapter 5		
Chapter 6		
Chapter 7		
Chapter 8		
Chapter 9		
Chapter 10		
Chapter 11		
Chapter 12		

From *Science & Stories,* published by GoodYearBooks. Copyright © 1994 Hilarie N. Staton and Tara McCarthy.

THE SCIENCE BEHIND THE TECHNOLOGY

LITERATURE:
The Twenty-one Balloons
William Péne du Bois (Puffin, 1986)

SCIENCE UNDERSTANDING:
Technological devices use a variety of scientific principles and concepts.

LITERARY GENRE:
Fantasy

BOOK SUMMARY:

The Twenty-one Balloons is the story of Professor Sherman's trip around the world. It is not a hard book, and has its own kind of silly humor. Professor Sherman is a teacher who retires to travel in a hydrogen-filled balloon. His adventures are framed with chapters that tell what happened after he was discovered floating in the Atlantic Ocean with a raft and twenty-one balloons. He refuses to tell his story until he reaches the Western American Explorers Club in San Francisco. So San Francisco prepares a balloon-filled gala to welcome him home. Once there, Professor Sherman tells his story.

The professor leaves San Francisco in his balloon in August 1883, but only gets partway across the Pacific before a seagull punctures his balloon. He barely makes it to land—and the closest land happens to be the island of Krakatoa with its very live volcano. As he wakens, he meets Mr. F, who becomes his guide to the incredible society built by twenty families on Krakatoa. Mr. F introduces the professor to Krakatoa's diamond mines, which supply the Krakatoans with money to do whatever they want. He introduces the families, who have changed their names to letters of the alphabet. Their houses and the food they serve reflect the culture of a country that begins with that letter.

Everyone on the island eats together, moving from one restaurant-house to another. The F's house is in French style, furnished with French furniture, and the F family serves French food on the day of the month that everyone eats at their house.

Mr. F describes the ways the families have adapted to the volcano, to their riches, and to living with each other. The professor sees the technological wonders of the M Family's home, of the children's Balloon Merry-Go-Round, and of the island's escape raft. Suddenly, the disastrous shuddering of the island indicates the volcano is getting ready to blow. Everyone races to the escape raft. They inflate its twenty-one balloons, and lift off, but are caught for a long time in the heat above the volcano. The raft frees itself only when the volcano momentarily calms down. Almost immediately, the volcano explodes (as did the real Krakatoa in 1883) and the raft begins a long journey west. Most of the families parachute into India, but since Professor Sherman doesn't have a parachute, he must wait until the raft is over water. The F family waits with him. Finally, he crashes into the Atlantic, thousands of miles from where he started. That's where a ship picks him up and the book begins.

PRE-READING

If you haven't used the introductory activity on page 75 to introduce technology, you might want to do it now.

1. Review the definitions of *technology* and discuss how it shapes the lives of students. Review the following scientific principles and concepts with students:

   • There are various forms of energy and these move through space and materials in various ways. (Cover mechanical energy, electrical energy, heat energy, and wind energy.)
   • Outside forces such as wind and gravity can act on a object to change its location, direction, and speed.
   • Different objects have different properties.

2. Invite students to give examples of how the concepts above can be applied to technology. A graphic like the following can be used to show how one principle might be found in a variety of technologies.

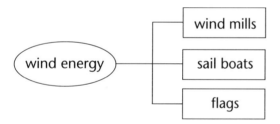

3. Introduce the book to students. Encourage them to predict what it might be about and how it might fit into their discussion of scientific principles. Read the first paragraph of the introduction. Discuss the two different attitudes toward travel that are mentioned here. Invite students to list all the real or imagined ways to travel by the shortest route or using the fastest method. Then do the same for the most roundabout route or more leisurely method. Discuss how descriptions of these two trips might differ. (amount of details, number of things seen, length, etc.) Have students share which way they'd like to travel if they had the chance.

BUILDING THE SCIENCE AND LITERATURE CONNECTION

Maybe because my sixth grade teacher, Miss Best, read this book aloud to us, I am recommending that you do the same. While you are reading the book, you can stop to discuss pertinent scientific principles or concepts or have small discussion groups cover these topics at the end of each chapter. The reading and questions can, of course, be made into a study guide for reading groups who are reading the book on their own rather than by the whole class.

Chapter 1. What are the different technologies used for communication in the story? (ship's log, newspaper, telegraph) What are the different technologies used for travel?

What type of energy do they rely upon? (giant balloon and 21 balloons—wind, motion; ship and train—steam power; carriage—horses)

Chapter 2. The author gives clear descriptions of how San Francisco decorated for Professor Sherman's arrival. Copy the description you like best and identify the most descriptive words in that section. From the author's descriptions and the events described, what are some properties of hydrogen? (Although the answers will vary, the fact that hydrogen is a light gas, floats, and will lift objects is important. Also, hydrogen is flammable.) What problems did hydrogen cause in San Francisco? (lifted children and rooftops; caused small fires and explosions) Predict how these characteristics might help or hinder a long trip in a hydrogen-filled balloon. (Answers will vary, but should be based on the answers to the above questions.)

Chapter 3. Predict problems Professor Sherman might have on his balloon trip. (Answers will vary, but might include problems with natural elements, birds, running out of supplies, control, etc.) How does the author describe Professor Sherman's balloon and living quarters? (Answers will vary, but should include details of what the basket and balloon look like, the functions of the different spaces, and how the Professor used the small space he had.) Design your own balloon. What would you take on a trip like the professor's?

Chapter 4. Tell how scientific principles involving wind, motion, friction, and weight played a part in ending Professor Sherman's trip. (Various answers are possible, depending on students' prior knowledge of the applicable scientific understandings. They could include motion through wind, action and reaction, correcting weight for lift, and friction between toes and water and body and sand.)

Chapter 5. The author uses description to let you know that life on this island is different than life in the rest of the world. Identify three of these descriptions and what they tell about Krakatoan life. (Answers will vary, but could include clothes, names, quaking land, and availability of supplies.) What are some properties of diamonds and volcanoes given in the story? Can you add others? (volcanoes—heat, lava, steam, earthquakes, etc; diamonds—hard, white, reflect light, worth a lot of money, etc.) How have the Krakatoans adapted to or changed the following parts of their environment: the volcano, the jungle, the diamonds?

(volcano—not changed, but must change to fit it, so they had to build their houses in a particular way, learn how to walk during quakes, etc.; jungle—cleared, used food from, kept as protection; diamonds—sun glasses, take what need, use as foundation of houses, etc.) What technology do they have or might they have used to create these changes or to make life on the island more pleasant? (Answers will vary, but could include tools for clearing, planting, mining, storage, etc.)

Chapter 6. List more ways the Krakatoans adapted to their environment. (Answers will vary, but could include how they built their homes and what they ate.) What problems did they have to solve before they adjusted to living peacefully together? (How to share equally and not be greedy.)

Chapter 7. Describe the technology that the M family used in their house. How did they use energy differently than other households? Give examples of the scientific principles they used in their technology. What would you invent if you were helping them prepare their house? (Answers will vary due to student interest and scientific background. They could include the steam engine, bed changer, and moving chairs. Transfer of energy, and action/reaction laws are some principles that can be applied.)

Chapter 8. The author gives clear descriptions of the Balloon-Merry-Go-Round. Identify three different descriptions that help you clearly visualize the Balloon-Merry-Go-Round and its trip. Identify the simple machines, rules of motion, and properties of heat and hydrogen that contributed to the Balloon-Merry-Go-Round and its trip with Professor Sherman. (Answers will vary depending on the students' prior knowledge, but the use of simple machines, such as the screw and wheel and axle should be included; action/reaction, wind and heat movement, and hydrogen's properties should be included too.)

Chapter 9. How and why have the Krakatoans adapted to the volcano when they a) go swimming in the ocean; and b) prepare an escape raft? (They sit in one place and let the water move over them. They know they can't control the volcano, so they must prepare for it to erupt.) What energy and forces did the Krakatoans have to consider when they built their escape raft? Predict problems that might occur when they try to use the escape raft. Identify some of the descriptive words that help you understand these problems. (Answers will vary, but the properties of hydrogen, transfer of energy and motion, weight, and balance should all be considered. Problems might include keeping level, changes in wind, inflating it fast enough, cinders, and control of speed and direction.)

Chapter 10. Identify three descriptions that help a reader understand that the raft's trip was not especially pleasant. What scientific principles controlled the movements of the raft: a) over the volcano; b) across the oceans and land; and c) coming down? (Answers will vary, but can include heat rises, winds are created by changes in temperature, winds flow in currents, it's hard to change direction while in a current, people become weaker with not enough food, and it is harder to run uphill than on a flat area.)

Evaluation. Have students create skits, summaries, or retellings of specific parts of the story. These can include the actual story line as well as the science that is involved in under-standing the story.

EXTENDING THE SCIENCE
Activity 1. Interested students might investigate how much weight can be carried by a regular balloon filled with helium by design-ing and carrying out a series of experiments with objects of varying weights and sizes tied to a balloon. Students can create charts summariz-ing their results and compare their conclusions to the information about hydrogen in the book.

Activity 2. Interested students can research volcanos and how their eruptions affect people. Their research might include weather changes, land changes (both addition and loss), and living conditions near the volcano. Students can share their information through a series of news broadcasts, "scientific" magazine articles, or imaginary personal accounts.

Activity 3. Students can create new designs for a Krakatoan house. Individuals or groups can build models or make an illustration of the building. In a written description, they can identify the scientific principles it uses and its practical uses. Encourage students to hold a technology show to share their designs with their classmates.

EXTENDING THE LITERATURE
Activity 1. Students might enjoy writing and giving illustrated tours of one of the Krakatoan houses. They can illustrate what they think they would see and discuss why things are they way they are.

Activity 2. Interested students can pretend they are Krakatoan children and write a journal about their lives. They can describe a normal day and how they feel about life on Krakatoa. Some students might want to write about their escape from Krakatoa instead. Encourage these students to include the technology they see and use on the island.

Activity 3. Students can research and write a newspaper article describing what really happened when Krakatoa erupted in 1883 and how it affected people. These can be gathered together and made into a newspaper.

From *Science & Stories*, published by GoodYearBooks. Copyright © 1994 Hilarie N. Staton and Tara McCarthy.

OTHER CONNECTIONS
GEOGRAPHY

Use a world map to trace Professor Sherman's two balloon voyages. Identify each country and ocean he crossed. Invite students to write an imaginative scene that shows how people might have reacted when they saw the huge balloon pass over them.

SOCIAL STUDIES

Divide the class into small groups and allow each group to choose a different letter and a country that begins with that letter. Encourage them to research the culture, especially the architecture and foods, of that country. They can design a Krakatoan "house-restaurant" that reflects that culture, create art reflecting the culture, and develop a day's menu using food from that culture. They can create an ad, poster, or elaborate menu for their restaurant to share with the class.

MATH

Create or have students create problems about the various things that can or can not be lifted by a balloon or set of balloons. Use the factual information about the balloons in the book (various display balloons in San Francisco lift 6, 60, and 75 pounds; balloons on the escape raft are either 16,200 or 32,400 cubic feet each; hydrogen's lifting power is 70 lbs per 1000 cubic feet) to create word problems such as the following:

> If the smaller balloons are 16,200 cubic feet each and the larger are 32,400 cubic feet each, how many smaller balloons will it take to lift the same amount as one of the large balloons?

TECHNOLOGY SOLVES EVERYDAY PROBLEMS

LITERATURE:
City: A Story of Roman Planning and Construction
David Macaulay (Houghton Mifflin Company, 1974)

SCIENCE UNDERSTANDING:
Technology has solved many problems and often becomes part of daily life.

LITERARY GENRE:
History

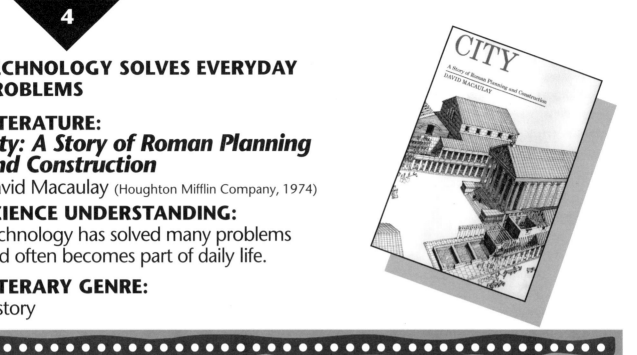

BOOK SUMMARY

City is a large book, filled with line drawings detailing the way the Romans planned and built a city. The clear text is not easy, but is brief and well supported by the pictures. Different drawings show birds'-eye views; people making decisions, working, and carrying on their daily lives; cutaway diagrams; and even architects' plans. Many processes are described, such as how Romans laid out the city, built roads and bridges, carried water great distances, and built houses, shops, temples, and theaters. Sanitation, baths, drinking water, and sewer systems are all described. Although the technology used to build walls, bridges, houses, and the amphitheater is discussed, the book is not just about the technology of building a city. It also describes life in the city, from where the shopping is done to what is shown in the theaters. Throughout the book, clear illustrations help students understand how technology worked before the age of fuel-powered machines. The city-building process is discussed chronologically, from before the city exists, to the first steps in planning, to life in the completed city.

PRE-READING

If you haven't done the unit introductory activity on page 75, which introduces students to technology in modern life, you may want to do that activity first.

1. Review the two definitions of *technology*. (non-natural objects of all kinds manufactured by people; and a system or process in which tools or machines and human power work together to increase people's ability to do tasks and thus change their environment) With students, compare how some changes are natural (such as land eroding from wind and rain) while similar ones are created by technology (such as land being moved by

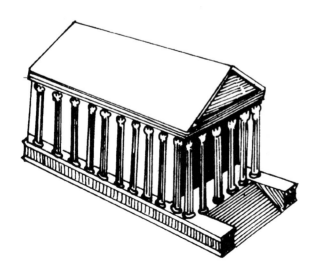

shovels or heavy equipment). Identify how a variety of scientific principles and concepts are applied in technology. Invite students to identify general areas where technology and science have worked together to solve problems, such as for better transportation, to improve human health and agriculture, and to end pollution.

2. Tell students they are going to be investigating how the Romans, who lived thousands of years ago, used science and technology to plan and build cities. Since the Romans lived before electricity, cars, trucks, and even trains, they used a simpler technology than we do today. Encourage students to predict (or recall if they have studied the Romans) what might be in a Roman city and how it might be built. Accept any reasonable answer, even if it is from a much less or much more advanced society.

3. Show the title page to students and ask what they think happened to the village. (It has been flooded.) Ask them how this flood might affect people many miles away in Rome. Compare it to the floods along the Mississippi River in 1993. Ask students to predict what the Romans might take into account before they build a large city near this site.

BUILDING THE SCIENCE AND LITERATURE CONNECTION

1. Form cooperative learning groups and have each one choose a different problem that the Romans solved with technology. The Study Guide has a list of some problems. Students can also suggest other problems from their previous discussions and prior knowledge.

2. If possible, have enough books so each group has one, but you may want to read the entire book to the whole class and discuss it as you go. As students read and review the book, have each group take notes

on the pertinent details. Encourage each group to discuss each section, using both the text and pictures to identify technology. Warn students most questions are dealt with throughout the book, not just in one section.

3. After the groups have completed the book, encourage them to write descriptions of how the Romans used technology to solve the problem they are investigating. They can create displays, diagrams, or models to illustrate part of their answer.

4. **Evaluation.** Have the class form into new groups. Groups do not need to include members from every research group, but each member of this new group should be from a different research group. Invite these groups to write about a person living, working, or visiting Verbonia. Their project can be a story, a diary, or a city tour. They should describe in detail the places, technology, and processes they see or take part in, using cues from the book.

EXTENDING THE SCIENCE

Activity 1. Interested students might like to build models or create comic strips of processes from the book. On the drawings, they can label the technologies and steps. Encourage students to present their projects at a technology fair.

Activity 2. Students can compare and contrast a specific process and its technology in Roman times to that same technology today. Students can create charts or illustrations to show the similarities and differences.

Activity 3. Ask students to identify some of the scientific principles and concepts behind a technological processes discussed in this book, such as building sewer systems or an aqueduct.

RECOMMENDED READING

Students might also enjoy reading *The Magic School Bus At The Waterworks*. Then they can compare and contrast health and technology issues in Roman and modern times. Students can create similar books about a trip to a Roman aqueduct, sewer system, or bath.

EXTENDING THE LITERATURE

Activity 1. Interested students might like to compare the descriptions in *The Twenty-one Balloons* about how the Krakatoans build their houses to the descriptions in this book about how the Romans built their buildings. Students can also compare Roman houses to modern houses.

Help students organize and write a three- or four-paragraph essay. Emphasize organizing facts before writing with a graph like one of the following:

```
┌──────────────────┐          ┌──────────────────┐
│   Paragraph 1    │          │   Paragraph 2    │
│  Details About   │───────▶  │  Details About   │
│  Roman Houses    │          │ Krakatoan Houses │
└──────────────────┘          └──────────────────┘
              │
              ▼
     ┌──────────────────┐
     │   Paragraph 3    │
     │ Differences Between │
     │ Roman and Krakatoan │
     │      Houses       │
     └──────────────────┘
```

```
        ( Introduction )
        ( Paragraph 1  )
         /            \
 ( Similarities )   ( Differences )
 ( Paragraph 2  )──▶( Paragraph 3 )
         \            /
        ( Conclusions )
        ( Paragraph 4 )
```

Activity 2. Suggest that students research and write introduction manuals for a technological process, such as building a sand castle or baking cookies. The manuals can be edited by other students who try to follow the directions. Their editing recommendations should encourage clear, concise, and sequential writing.

Activity 3. Students might like to write, rewrite, or reorganize one description from the book that they feel was too skimpy or unclear.

OTHER CONNECTIONS
ART

While you show students pictures of Roman mosaics, discuss the patterns and pictures used. Identify appropriate pictures that might be used in specific locations, like a dolphin in a bathing pool. Invite students to create their own mosaic pictures by using small squares of paper to create pictures. Hold an art show of these mosaics.

SOCIAL STUDIES

Reread the book *City* to identify clues about Roman life. Students can research Roman life further using books such as Jonathan Rutland's *See Inside a Roman Town* or Rupert Matthew's biography of Julius Caesar. Encourage students to compare their daily life today with that of a Roman person. They can present one segment of their findings as a play, mural, or interview.

STUDY GUIDE TIPS

1. Remind students to note the book page numbers and titles of any other sources they use as they tell about the problem and its related technology.

2. As a concluding activity, you might have students review the list of problems and identify any that are *not* problems for people today. Though discussion, most students will see that the problems are constants throughout history, and so apply to their own communities as well as those in Roman times.

From *Science & Stories*, published by GoodYearBooks. Copyright © 1994 Hilarie N. Staton and Tara McCarthy.

City: A Story of Roman Planning and Construction

Name: _____ Date: _____

As a group, choose one of the following daily living problems and identify the technology the Romans used to solve it.

People needed fresh water.

People wanted to easily travel long and short distances.

People needed to get food and supplies from far away.

People needed to safely cross large rivers.

People needed food to live.

People needed to protect their city, homes, and goods.

People needed to keep clean.

People wanted entertainment.

People wanted a variety of goods to buy.

People wanted to live in beautiful places.

_____

_____

_____

_____

_____

_____

_____

_____

_____

_____

_____

TECHNOLOGY'S AFFECT ON SOCIETY

LITERATURE:
Lyddie
Katherine Paterson (Penguin Books, 1991)

SCIENCE UNDERSTANDING:
Technological changes can create changes in a society

LITERARY GENRE:
Historical fiction

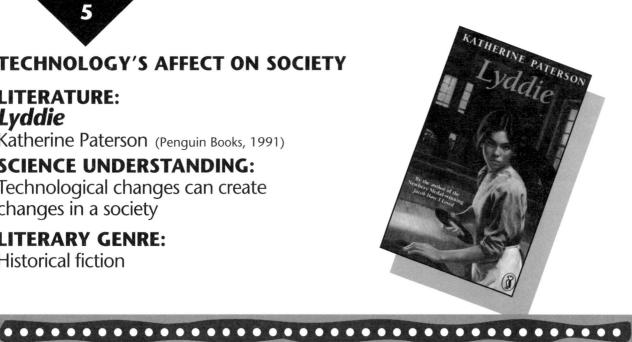

From *Science & Stories*, published by GoodYearBooks. Copyright © 1994 Hilarie N. Staton and Tara McCarthy.

BOOK SUMMARY:

Lyddie is a high-level book, but is extremely well written. The technology, science, and societal changes are well integrated into the story of this proud, intelligent person. The story also deals with strong themes about family, poverty, and social class. The story of Lyddie's development is complex, but very human.

Lyddie is a poor farm girl in 1840s Vermont. Her father has left home and her mother is escaping from reality, which leaves young Lyddie and her brother, Charles, to provide for her mother and two younger sisters. After her mother and sisters move away to stay with family, Lyddie and Charles cope well, until their mother decides that Charles will work at a mill and Lyddie at a tavern to earn money to pay off the farm's debt. Sadly they leave, talking of when they and their father will return.

Lyddie is introduced to new people and new ideas at the tavern, but sees herself as trapped like a slave. She decides to go to Lowell, Massachusetts, where she gets work in a textile mill. In Lowell, Lyddie makes a variety of friends: Betsy, who loves learning and introduces Lyddie to reading, Dickens, and Oberlin College; Amelia, who is religious; Diana, a political "radical" who trains Lyddie in the complex process of running the loom; and Brigid, an Irish immigrant Lyddie first resents and then accepts as a close friend. At the mill, Lyddie must learn to cope with the loud noise, heat, frightening machines, a lecherous overseer, the health problems of her friends, and her own fear of the immigrant workers. She pushes herself very hard, both in the job and in learning to read. She hoards her money and takes little time for anything else.

Then Lyddie's uncle appears to tell her that her mother has been placed in an asylum and that he is leaving Lyddie's remaining sister, Rachel, with her. At that point, Lyddie becomes very ill and is unable to work for a long time. When she finally returns to work, Rachel begins working at the mill too. Rachel soon develops a bad cough, like many of the other workers, but is saved when their brother Charles appears and takes Rachel away to join his new, kind family. Left alone by her sister and roommates who have either married or developed bad health, Lyddie begins to reconsider her decision to stay out of the labor protests. She talks to Diana, only to find that she, too, is leaving because she is having a child out of wedlock. Lyddie ends up losing her job because she defends her Irish friend, Brigid, from the overseer's improper advances.

She threatens the overseer with exposure to save Brigid's job, but takes the chance to leave. Lyddie visits Diana, returns to the tavern and to the farm, but fits nowhere. Woven throughout the story is the silent Quaker boy and his family who lived near Lyddie's farm. He asks her to marry him, but instead, she decides to go to Oberlin College and maybe someday return to him.

PRE-READING

If you haven't used the unit introductory activity on page 75, you might want to use it to introduce students to how technology is a part of their everyday lives.

1. Encourage students to identify problems that are solved with technology, such as cooking food, remaining warm in cold weather (both inside and outside), and getting places easily and quickly.

2. Review the students' list of things they use that have been made possible by technology (from the unit introductory activity). Invite groups of students to categorize the items into various technological levels (less advanced to most advanced). The number of categories can be determined by the abilities of your students, but at least three should be used. Have them share their categories with the class and allow them to justify any placements that class members question.

3. Encourage students to draw on their history background to describe life on a Northeastern farm in the early-to-mid 1800s. As their descriptions proceed, have

volunteers identify the technology being used and determine whether they would categorize it as less or more advanced technology. As students offer phrases, encourage them to use exact words that help create how people feel. They might use terms such as back-breaking plowing, boring churning, or scary hunting.

4. Introduce the book to students by telling them it is about a girl who goes from a less technologically advanced farm to a more technologically advanced factory. Invite them to predict what new technology she will encounter, how it will change her life, what problems the new technology might create, and what attitudes Lyddie and the people she meets will have about the changing technology. Write the predictions down for students to consider after they have completed the book.

BUILDING THE SCIENCE AND LITERATURE CONNECTION

1. Since *Lyddie* is a complex book, you might want to read it to students or have individuals read it. A longer reading guide can be compiled to focus students reading on the story rather than on the technology. Hand out the Lyddie Study Guide to students. Discuss the chart and the questions with students. Read the first four paragraphs of the book to students. Invite them to identify the technology and the category each would fit into. (lowest technology: fire; less advanced technology: door that doesn't close, pot, ladder) Remind them to think in terms of 1843 technology, not today's technology. Teach or review note-taking techniques for students who need it. As students reach natural stopping points in their reading, have them compare and discuss their lists with other class members.

2. Make a copy of the following chart and show it to students:

Problem	Technology	Changes to environment and life (good and bad)
slow travel	trains	faster travel, smoke and cinders, expensive, more jobs, danger to workers, move freight and people faster and farther, only goes where there are tracks, more room to sit, more people in accidents

3. Have the group choose five items from their more- or most-advanced technology lists or their mill technology list and use their choices to create a problem chart like the one above.

4. Katherine Paterson uses a variety of words to create moods and to reveal the feelings of the characters in her book. For instance, she writes, "Diana's laugh was short and harsh." These clear and specific words give readers a mental picture of how Diana felt. After you introduce this concept to students, invite them to locate other examples of words that reveal a character's feelings.

5. Have students go back to their chart of changes and use its information to write and rehearse a scene which shows the feelings of two or more people toward the changes caused by one or more types of technology. Encourage them to use specific, mood-building and feeling-exposing language. As they are rehearsing their scenes, recommend they use speaking and acting techniques to further enhance the mood, such as tone of voice and body language. Encourage them to revise and rehearse their scene so that the language and presentation create a clear message about the feelings of the characters.

6. **Evaluation.** Students can return to the survey of technology in the unit opening activity, and compare their results and conclusions with the feeling of the people

in *Lyddie.* Encourage them to make generalizations about how people feel about technology and change.

EXTENDING THE SCIENCE
Activity 1. Suggest that students investigate and build a working waterwheel, loom, or grist mill. Students can experiment with various relationships of simple machines to create a complex machine or system. Invite them to display their projects during a technology fair.

Activity 2. Students interested in energy or history might enjoy investigating mills and how the energy of the running water is transferred to the looms (or to the grindstones of a flour mill). Once the research is done, they can make diagrams or charts with labels and scientific descriptions for each section. These can be displayed around the room for all to learn from.

Activity 3. Students can choose another form of technology in the book and create models or charts of it and how it uses energy and how it does work. Encourage students to identify the various scientific principles used by each and the various changes in that process or machine since Lyddie's time.

EXTENDING THE LITERATURE
Activity 1. Interested students might like to write a journal for Lyddie or one of her room-mates, which tells about life at the mill. They

From *Science & Stories*, published by GoodYearBooks. Copyright © 1994 Hilarie N. Staton and Tara McCarthy.

can include events from the book or new ones created by the students, but all should fit the personality of the characters. Encourage students to use words that not only describe what is happening but also describe and discuss the feelings and moods of the people.

Activity 2. For interested or more advanced students, read Charles Dickens's description of the Lowell mills in his book *American Notes.* Discuss with students what the characters meant about these descriptions being romantic and what words they'd change to create less romantic and more realistic descriptions. Then have them write and share their own descriptions to better create the mood of the girls who worked at the Lowell mills.

OTHER CONNECTIONS
MUSIC
Diana's group was protesting the working conditions at the mill. Encourage students to identify other times and places people have protested working conditions. Play some protest songs for students, such as those of Heddy West (on Folk Legacy recording label) or from the collections published by the Smithsonian Folkways label. Although most protest songs are about later movements, students can compare the types of demands being made with those being made by the

textile mill girls in the book. Small groups of students can write their own protest verses to common tunes. Their topics can be modern injustices, the Lowell mills, or even school life. Encourage them to share their songs, either in written form or by singing them to the class.

GEOGRAPHY/MATH
After providing a road map of Ohio to the Atlantic coast, help students identify or put on the map: Burlington and another small town in Vermont (since the specific location of Lyddie's family farm is not given); Lowell and Boston, Massachusetts; and Oberlin, Ohio (near Cleveland). Using the map's mileage scale, encourage students to determine the mileage of the various trips discussed in the book. In a discussion, identify the modern ways to travel these routes, and have students create problems comparing the time necessary for the same trip in 1846 and today.

DRAMA
Invite students to do a reader's theater with key scenes from the book (i.e., riding in the stage, using the looms, cooking on a stove, or riding the train). Suggest they pantomime the use of the machines, such as the looms. Encourage students to use tone of voice to emphasize key words and phrases as they are reading.

SOCIAL STUDIES
Encourage student to recall important technological developments that changed American society from the 1790s until the 1850s. Be sure the students identify technology that was important in the development of their own area, such as steel plows, cotton gins, trains, canals, or steamboats. Have small groups each review a different type of technology and determine the ways it affected people living at that time. Encourage them to list both positive and negative effects.

1. Answers will vary, so remind students to list page numbers to show where they found the information. Some sample answers are:

Transportation
- less advanced: walking, riding horses
- more advanced: stage coaches
- most advanced: train

Food
- less advanced: raw food, gathering what was needed from woods
- more advanced: cooking food in fireplace
- most advanced: cooking on metal stove

Cloth Making
- less advanced: animal skins
- more advanced: cloths made at home
- most advanced: factory-made cloth

2. Students could list and describe the heating system, the looms, or the water power.

3. Students should be able to make the generalization that some people used technology for their own gains, others to make life more comfortable for themselves, and others didn't want anything to do with advanced technology.

From *Science & Stories*, published by GoodYearBooks. Copyright © 1994 Hilarie N. Staton and Tara McCarthy.

Lyddie

Name: _____ Date: _____

As you read *Lyddie,* take notes to fill in the chart and answer the questions below.

1. On this chart write the technology that Lyddie uses or encounters. Write each under the appropriate category and type of technology.

	Less Advanced Technology	More Advanced Technology	Most Advanced Technology
Transportation			
Food Growing and Preparing			
Cloth Making			

2. What type of technology was used at the mill? Describe one of the machines or systems that was used.

_____

_____

_____

3. Choose two characters in the story, like Lyddie, the mill owner, or Triphena. Tell how each felt about the more and most advanced technology.

_____

_____

_____

SPACE

SCIENCE UNDERSTANDINGS

In this unit, students explore the night sky, our solar system, and space travel. In the process of this exploration, students develop the following understandings, which are linked to the science curriculums of the intermediate grades:

1. The universe encompasses great distances.

2. The planets of our solar system have unique characteristics.

3. Scientists study and test ideas in a variety of ways.

4. Technology allows people to explore and exist in space.

UNIT MAP

Each lesson revolves around one or more pieces of children's literature, emphasizes a literary genre or literary strategy, and focuses on a problem students can solve as they work through the lesson.

Lesson	Literature	Genre/Strategy	Problem
1	**Star Tales: North American Indian Stories About the Stars**	Myths	Why does the light of some stars appear brighter than others?
2	**Galileo**	Biography	How do scientists test ideas? What is the relationship between the sun, the earth, and the moon?
3	**Journey to the Planets**	Nonfiction	What are the characteristics of the planets in our solar system?
4	**To Space and Back**	Personal account	How can people live in space?
5	**The Package in Hyperspace**	Science fiction	What unique problems do people have to solve during space travel?

From *Science & Stories*, published by GoodYearBooks. Copyright © 1994 Hilarie N. Staton and Tara McCarthy.

INTRODUCING THE SPACE UNIT

1. Ask students what they think of when they hear the word *space*. Encourage a variety of definitions (a blank or empty area; a reserved or available accommodation on public transportation; an area provided for a particular purpose, etc.). Define *space* as they will be studying it in this unit. (the expanses in which the solar system, stars and galaxies exist—the universe) You can further refine the concept by adding that outer space is defined as space outside our atmosphere.

2. Once everyone is sure what you are talking about, ask students to recall what they know about space. Write facts on a chart under the heading "What We Know About Space." If anyone questions a fact, write it under the heading "What We Think We Know About Space." Finally, ask students to think of questions they'd like to go under the heading "What We'd Like to Learn About Space." Ask students to copy the chart and refer to it during the unit.

3. As soon as the chart is complete, ask students to identify where they have learned about space and where they could learn more about it. Encourage them to include science texts, magazines, and newspapers as well as stories, movies, and television shows—both documentaries and science fiction.

4. Have a variety of newspapers, magazines, and a *Farmer's Almanac* available. Form small groups of three or four students and give each group a selection of these materials. Have them search for all mentions of space, stars, planets, and other words they think are related to the topic. After they've scanned all the materials, encourage groups to share their findings and to categorize the different information. General categories might include space travel, satellites, and the moon's phases. Encourage students to add facts and questions to their charts.

INTRODUCING THE SYNTHESIS ACTIVITY

If you are going to use the unit's synthesis activity, you might want to introduce students to it now so they can think about it while they work on their unit.

1. Write the activity's objective (see below) on the chalkboard and underline the phrases "on another planet," "in space," and "specific scientific principles." Tell students they will be reading a variety of fiction and nonfiction books about space. Discuss how they might be able to use what they learn about the scientific principles that apply on various planets and that apply to travel in space. Point out that they will be able to use these principles to develop stories and characters.

2. Have students form the cooperative learning groups that will do the final activity. They can meet periodically throughout the unit to discuss scientific principles and locales they might want to include in their final science fiction story.

3. Individual students or cooperative groups can develop portfolios using all the activities done during the unit. They can draw on that information for their final activity and for assessment.

CARRYING OUT THE UNIT SYNTHESIS ACTIVITY

The final activity is a synthesis activity which allows students to use what they have learned in both the science program and from the literature to create something that incorporates their knowledge into a major project about space and our relation to it.

> **Objective.** To write a science fiction story which takes place on another planet and is based on specific scientific principles with characters adapted to or adapting to their environment and who solve problems related to their environment.

Step 1. Review the chart the class made at the beginning of the unit. Create a revised version by cutting the old chart up and rearranging the items. Add new items and encourage students to identify still unanswered questions. Some of these can be researched by students, while others might need to be identified as not yet answerable by science.

Step 2. Divide the class into partners or small groups. Some students may want to work independently at this project. Each group will be responsible for writing a science fiction story based on accurate scientific ideas. Suggest students create a story map before they begin to write. The information on this map should include details about the following:

- the setting, which can be in a spaceship or on a specific planet. The details must be based on scientific facts about gravity, atmosphere, physical characteristics, and possible or plausible technology.
- the characters, especially aliens, should be described with physical features, needs, emotions, and attitudes. Students should include their reasons for giving their aliens specific features. For instance, the aliens might have eyes the size of saucers so their large pupils can see in low light levels.
- problems to be solved and attempted and final solutions along with the major events. As the story takes form, these events can be sequenced and the climax noted.

All these plot elements should be consistent with scientific principles, especially those stressed in this unit. After students have planned their stories in detail, encourage each group member to write one section of the story, or assign various roles (writer, editor, illustrator, and so forth).

INTEGRATION ACTIVITIES

These connection activities can be done while the students are reading any of the books or after they have completed the books or unit. These activities connect the general unit theme to other content areas in especially creative ways.

HISTORY

Over the course of the unit, create a class timeline of how people have viewed space, from earliest times to present day. Students can include pictures to represent myths, theories about space and the heavens, stars as directional guides, astronomy, astrology, and space exploration. Encourage them to draw the conclusion that most of what we learned has been in the past 100 years and the amount of knowledge gained in the past 20 years has exceeded everything that went before.

ART

To introduce students to artists' views of space and space travel, display paintings and illustrations that show the stars, space travel, planet environments, and various related subjects. Include famous paintings such as Van Gogh's *Starry Night,* science fiction paperback covers, and even Christmas cards (for examples of stars). Invite students to compare these emotional illustrations with real science photographs or illustrations (contact NASA or the Smithsonian's Air and Space Museum for some of these).

MUSIC

A recent genre of music has been labeled "space music" because it evokes the aura of space. Play some for students and ask them to describe what they imagine as they listen to the music. Remind them listening to music is an intensely personal experience and what a person sees and feels may be very different from what other people experience. Invite students to draw pictures that illustrate what the music is trying to convey and the feelings it evokes. Other students may want to express their feelings in terms of dance or mime.

From *Science & Stories*, published by GoodYearBooks. Copyright © 1994 Hilarie N. Staton and Tara McCarthy.

ADDITIONAL MATERIALS

For additional materials you might want to use with this unit, see Additional Resources, pages 130-134.

OBSERVING THE HEAVENS

LITERATURE:
Star Tales: North American Indian Stories About the Stars
Gretchen Will Mayo
(Walker Publishing Company, 1987)

SCIENCE UNDERSTANDING:
The light of stars is affected by distance, brightness, size, the earth's atmosphere, or any of these in combination.

LITERARY GENRE:
Myths

From *Science & Stories*, published by GoodYearBooks. Copyright © 1994 Hilarie N. Staton and Tara McCarthy.

BOOK SUMMARIES

Star Tales recounts sixteen Native American short stories about the stars, from a variety of tribes and oral traditions. The introduction pages scattered throughout the book often identify the tribes, stars, and traditions that gave birth to the stories. The stories include the Pawnee's "Adventure Along the White River in the Sky," which tells how a village rescues Canoemaker from the sky while Robin and Beaver steal fire for humans. All escape from the sky, but leave their arrows as the Milky Way. In the Umatilla Chinook's "The Race for the Prize Fish," the Cold North Wind and the Chinook Wind fight and prove that the strongest won't necessarily win. The Ojibwa's tale "The Birds of Summer" tells how Fisher brought back the Birds of Summer from Cruel-Face and then escaped into the winter sky.

PRE-READING

If you have not introduced space to students with the unit opening activity (page 103), you might want to do so now.

1. Give each of three students a flashlight of a different intensity. Send them to one end of the room, while the rest of the class stands at the other end. Tell the class they are going to pretend it is night and they are looking at the stars in the night sky. Before you turn out the lights, warn students not to look directly into the lights and discuss how the light can harm their vision. With the lights out, ask the class to identify which is brighter. Invite students to rearrange the location of the lights several times to form a variety of patterns with the lights at a variety of distances from the class.

2. Ask the class what they might do if they had to remember the pattern of lights (name them, connect them into a pattern, make a story around them). Define a *constellation* for students (a group of stars that seem to form a particular shape). Ask them what they think stars are (distant suns) and how we can see them (light travels great distances through space).

3. Encourage students to recall or predict the type of things early cultures might have seen in the stars. Also have them hypothesize why these cultures might tell stories about the stars (to make them less frightening, to

remember their location for direction, and so forth). Ask students what these types of stories are called (myths) and invite a few students to retell a myth. Don't define myths—save that for after students have read the book.

BUILDING THE SCIENCE AND LITERATURE CONNECTION

1. Divide the class into small groups. Have each group practice one or two myths to present to the class. They can do them as choral readings, reader's theater, or storytelling scenes. Encourage students to analyze the types of stories that are being told. From their analysis, create a definition of a *myth*. (Myths tell about the creation of something important to a people, like the cosmos or a way of life. They take place in an earlier, unidentifiable time.)

2. Remind students of the activity they did with the flashlights. As a whole class, or in their groups, allow students to conduct a short investigation into the factors that determine how bright a star is to us on the earth. Give them the Investigation Guide, and explain the procedure. After they have completed their Investigation Guides, show the whole class a large, clear bowl of water between the flashlight and the viewer so that they can identify the effects of the earth's atmosphere on light from distant suns. (The atmosphere bends, spreads, and distorts the light.)

3. After students have completed the investigation, hold a class discussion to generalize their results and the scientific principles that apply to the stars. You can also introduce the color and temperature relationships of stars (hot—red; hotter—yellow; hottest—blue-white). Our sun and other yellow suns are about 5,700° Celsius. Red stars are cooler and blue-white ones are hotter. Invite students to predict what would happen if our sun changed either to a red sun or to a blue-white sun.

4. Have students return to their groups. Pass out the star maps and have each group "see a picture" in the stars and identify their own constellation. After they have chosen one, they can create a myth about how that constellation came to be. Once they have their constellation and myth, each member of the group can take a different task to prepare for the presentation of their constellation and myth to the class.

- Cut a black construction circle a little larger than an round cardboard oatmeal box. Punch holes in the paper to represent a constellation. Vary the intensity of the stars by varying the size of the holes. Tape the paper to one end of the container and shine a flashlight through it from the other end. When this is projected on a wall in a darkened room, the constellation will appear. Students can also make star maps of their constellations that show how the stars are joined or related to the story they decided upon.

THE LYRE

UP

- Write the myth the group has agreed upon. Use other group members as editors.
- Illustrate the myth.
- Choose one star in their constellation and research its name, distance from the earth, color, and anything else that can be found about it.

5. **Evaluation.** After all the students have completed their constellation projects, invite them to present their projects to the class. Have students assess the presentations for their scientific accuracy, presentation skill, or artistry.

6. Collect all the myths, illustrations, and star maps in a class constellation mythology book.

EXTENDING THE SCIENCE

Activity 1. Students might want to investigate how the night sky changes during the year and create a demonstration for the class that explains the process. They might make use of the techniques students used in their Building the Science Connection Activity.

Activity 2. Students might enjoy taking photographs of the night sky, if they are where the atmosphere and lights don't obliterate the stars. Use a camera with a cable release and loaded with fast film, set up on a tripod, and left with its shutter wide open. Pictures taken at various intervals (shutter open for 30 seconds, 1 minute, 15 minutes, etc.) will show different numbers of stars (longer exposures allow more light to hit the film). Very long exposures (five to six hours) will show the way the stars move through the night sky. A display of these photos, with appropriate captions, can be used to create a class bulletin board.

Activity 3. Students might enjoy investigating the technology humans used to learn about the universe. Reflecting telescopes, refracting telescopes, radio telescopes, the Hubble telescope and space probes can each be the focus of a group's research. They can identify how technology has changed over the years.

EXTENDING THE LITERATURE
Activity. Students might want to locate, read, and write myths and legends that explain other natural phenomena that relate to space, such as full moons, lunar or solar eclipses, shooting stars, seasons, and tides.

ADDITIONAL READING
Students can locate, practice, and present to the class poetry that uses the stars and the night sky for its subject matter. Encourage students to find all types from nursery rhymes to haiku and sonnets. Students who are interested can also write their own poetry.

OTHER CONNECTIONS
STORYTELLING
Invite students to memorize some of the myths they've read or written. Encourage them to embellish and dramatize the myth, while keeping true to the story. Students might want to make costumes so that they feel "authentic" as they tell their myths. Make arrangements through other teachers or the librarian for a storytelling day where various students tell their myths to younger students.

MATH
Divide the class into partners and give each set a one-inch string. Then have them measure some large area (i.e., auditorium, ball field, outside of school building, or a square acre of land) using that string as a measure. When they return, have them discuss the huge number they got and what measurement could be used instead. Tell students that scientists had the same problem when measuring distances to the stars and have solved it by creating a huge measure: the light year. This is the distance light travels in one year: 6 trillion miles or 10 trillion kilometers. Invite volunteers to write this number on the chalkboard. Then have groups of students locate the distances between different stars and make graphs and word problems using the information they've located.

HISTORY
Invite students to investigate the part stars have played in navigation. Groups can investigate how different seafaring people (such as the Arabs, Columbus, and the Portuguese) used the stars as a guide. They can write captain's log entries to show how the stars were used and how much the captain depended upon them.

From *Science & Stories*, published by GoodYearBooks. Copyright © 1994 Hilarie N. Staton and Tara McCarthy.

From *Science & Stories*, published by GoodYearBooks. Copyright © 1994 Hilarie N. Staton and Tara McCarthy.

STUDY GUIDE TIPS

Answers will vary, but be sure students identify the following generalizations:

- The farther a light has to travel the dimmer it will be.

- A larger, bright light will remain brighter if its light must travel the same distance and go through the same atmosphere.

- A closer, less bright star might seem brighter because its light travels less distance.

Star Tales: North American Indian Stories About the Stars

Name: _____ Date: _____

STAR INVESTIGATION GUIDE

With your group do each of the following procedures and then evaluate what you see.

1. Number three flashlights of different sizes #1, #2, and #3. Fill in the size in this list.

   #1 is the _____ flashlight

   #2 is the _____ flashlight.

   #3 is the _____ flashlight.

2. Place the flashlights side by side exactly the same distance from the viewers. Turn them on. List them with the brightest first:

   Brightest_____

   Bright _____

   Least bright _____

3. Move the two smaller flashlights closer and view them again. Sketch your investigation. List them in order of brightness.

   Brightest_____

   Bright _____

   Least bright _____

4. Move the smallest, dimmest light much closer. Sketch the scene and view the lights again. List them in order of brightness.

   Brightest_____

   Bright _____

   Least bright _____

5. Use the other side of this page to answer these questions.

   a. How has distance affected how bright the lights seem to you?

   b. Does the size of the light play any part in how bright the light seems to you? Give your evidence in thinking this.

   c. Does this hold true no matter where the lights are placed?

   d. Write a generalization about the intensity of stars. Refer to its size, brightness, and distance from the earth.

From *Science & Stories*, published by GoodYearBooks. Copyright © 1994 Hilarie N. Staton and Tara McCarthy.

LESSON 2

INVESTIGATING THE SUN, THE MOON, AND THE EARTH

LITERATURE:
Galileo
Leonard Everett Fisher
(Macmillan Publishing Company, 1992)

SCIENCE UNDERSTANDING:
Scientists test ideas with various techniques before they accept them as true. The relationship between the sun, the earth, and the moon causes various natural events.

LITERARY GENRE:
Biography

BOOK SUMMARY

Galileo is a short biography of the man called "the father of science." The book's 13 double-page spreads include one large black and white illustration with a moderate amount of text. The text uses vocabulary that might be unfamiliar to students, so although this looks like a "picture book," it is much more advanced.

The book tells how Galileo Galilei's poor family sent him to the best schools to learn medicine and then the sciences. Galileo spent much of his life trying to prove the ideas of the astronomer Copernicus (the planets revolve around the sun, not the earth) and protecting himself from the Roman Catholic Church (which was reacting to the Reformation with the Inquisition). Galileo's other observations covered a wide variety of topics and resulted in or verified many scientific ideas about pendulums, gravity, and magnets. He also applied science to invent or improve technology. He built themoscopes (thermometers), telescopes, and microscopes. Galileo's observations of the heavens verified Copernicus's theory and earned the condemnation of the Roman Catholic Church. These observations included the physical features of the moon, Jupiter's moons in orbit, what he thought were stars circling Saturn, and sunlight moving across Venus.

The book does not ignore the jealousy, outrage, and fear of churchmen, professors, and princes, which culminated when Galileo is called before the Holy Office of the Inquisition. The book states: "His crime was thought worse than the offenses of Martin Luther." Little is said of his ordeal, but Galileo is suddenly portrayed as sick, exhausted, and without the previous supports he enjoyed. Although he had previously accused the Church of ignoring the truth, he signed a paper saying he was wrong. In spite of being crushed by the Church and by his daughter's death, he continued his work on force and motion. Even after he became blind he continued to verify ideas. What Galileo learned allowed others, like Sir Isaac Newton, to discover important laws of gravity and motion. The Roman Catholic Church did not officially accept his findings about the solar system as truth until 1979.

PRE-READING

If you have not used the unit introductory activity (page 103) to help students define space and to gather their prior knowledge, you might want to do so now.

1. Ask students to recall all the scientists they've encounter in their studies and to list all the ways scientists learn about things. Encourage students to include processes such as observation, experimentation, and asking questions.

2. Ask students to pretend they live in a much earlier time and in a place where many scientific principles are just being discovered. Comment on how some people fear that these new ideas will destroy their way of life or religion, so they refuse to listen to the information. Encourage students to predict the problems a scientist who is trying to prove these new ideas would have. Ask students if they can recall examples of scientists and scientific ideas being treated like this. (Darwin and evolution, the early industrial revolution, introduction of electricity, microwaves, or computers)

3. While holding up the book *Galileo*, have students predict what this scientist is know for and what troubles and problems he might encounter during his life.

BUILDING THE SCIENCE AND LITERATURE CONNECTION

This book can be used as a springboard to a variety of demonstrations or you can use only those dealing with the solar system.

1. Read the book to students. After each page of text, stop, define the unknown terms, explain confusing historical situations, and discuss the following questions.

After Page 2 (first page of text). How did Copernicus' ideas differ from Aristotle's ideas? Why did Galileo's ideas upset the Roman Catholic Church? (Aristotle and the Church believed the earth was the center of the universe and everything revolved around it. Copernicus believed the earth and planets revolved around the sun. The church didn't like anyone teaching ideas opposed to its own ideas.) Predict some problems Galileo might have when he tries to prove Copernicus' theory was right. (Answers will vary depending on knowledge of students, but they should be able to predict problems with the Roman Catholic Church.)

After Pages 6 and 8. What questions might Galileo have asked himself as he saw the pendulum swinging? (Answers will vary, but should include questions concerning the components of a pendulum such as: Does the length of the rope matter? or What would happen if I changed the weight?) What do you think the law of the pendulum says? (Answers will vary, but the law says the period of the pendulum's swing does not depend upon the length or its size.) How did Galileo's ideas influence the rest of the world? (People used his ideas, like the pendulum, to create new technology.)

After Pages 10 and 12. What questions might Galileo have asked when he challenged Aristotle's theories about falling objects? (Answers will vary, but should include the components of weight and speed.) What new questions might Galileo ask about temperature once he knew that it could be measured? (Answers will vary, but could include questions about why objects get hot or cool at different rates.) What questions about magnets and magnetism do you think Galileo and his students might ask and investigate? (Answers will vary, but might include what causes magnetism and what are the characteristics of objects attracted to magnets.)

After Pages 14, 16, and 18. What influences lead Galileo to his discoveries

From *Science & Stories*, published by GoodYearBooks. Copyright © 1994 Hilarie N. Staton and Tara McCarthy.

about the moon's surface? (new technology, Copernicus) What new questions did his discoveries raise? Which have we answered since 1609? (Many answers are possible, but could include questions about the moon's surface, how stars are formed, Saturn's stars, and orbits. Many have been answered since 1609.) How have we proven Galileo was correct about the moon? What technology have we used? How has this technology changed since Galileo's time? (Answers should include information about the space programs, walking on the moon, and advanced telescopes.)

After Page 20. What new questions might Galileo have asked after he saw the sunspots? (Answers will vary but should include questions about causation.) Why might the Roman Catholic Church have taken such a firm stand against Galileo and his findings? (Answers will vary, but should include the prior information that it felt its basic beliefs were being attacked.) What words and phrases does the author use to identify how upset the Pope, the Roman Catholic Church, and other people were with his ideas. (Answers will vary, but should include verbs and adjectives that describe their emotions and stance, such as enraged and once friendly.)

After Pages 22, 24, and 26. How did Galileo influence others in Europe during his lifetime? (published books, new laws, developed new technology, challenged old beliefs) What people and events most influenced Galileo as he got older? How did this change his life? (Answers will vary but should include Church's attack on him, the loss of his supporters and family, and his poor health and blindness. These changed his life, but not his continuing search for truth.)

2. After you have finished reading the book, discuss the historical and scientific ideas and how they apply to their life today.

3. **Evaluation.** Divide students into small groups. Ask them to write letters to Galileo to tell him what science has learned about

the sun, the moon and the earth since his death in 1642. Each member of the group should choose one area (such as the earth's orbit, lunar surface, or sunspots) and research the current information on that topic and how we obtained it. Tell students you will evaluate their research, factual content, and clear presentation. After each group member contributes a paragraph or two to a group letter to Galileo, invite them to share their letters with the class.

EXTENDING THE SCIENCE
Activity 1. Students might like to test Galileo's ideas on various scientific laws and concepts. Students can divide into groups, each with a different idea to explore and test. They can design their own investigation of the ideas in this book and then share their results with the class. Some principles Galileo worked on are the following:

- The period of a pendulum (time through arc and back) does not depend upon the length of its size (as the arc gets smaller, the speed slows, so it continues to take the same time).
- All objects fall at the same speed.
- All objects fall the same distance in the same time unless acted on by outside forces.
- An object moves freely until something happens to stop it or make it change direction.
- Heat is the motion of tiny particles. All objects are made of these tiny particles.
- Forces act independently on a body.
- There is a relationship between an action and reaction.
- Buoyancy is the upward force exerted on an immersed or floating object by a liquid.

Activity 2. Students might like to create sundials. You will need to locate the angle for the triangle that is appropriate for your latitude. Excellent instructions and appropriate triangles are given in *Ranger Rick's NatureScope; Astronomy Adventures.* Students can check the accuracy of their sundials by making readings at specific times each day over a week or so.

Activity 3. Students might like to investigate what people have learned about the moon's surface. They can identify whether the findings were from advanced telescopes, satellites, or visits to the moon. Suggest that students create and teach a lunar geography lesson to the class with their own visuals, charts, maps, and models.

EXTENDING THE LITERATURE

Activity 1. Interested students might like to pretend they are living at the time of Galileo. They can write letters or newspaper editorials which either encourage Galileo to continue or call for him to abandon his investigations. Students can conduct a debate in which both sides of the controversy are well represented.

Activity 2. Students can write clear descriptions of an experiment or observation that might have been used by Galileo to test one of his ideas. Students should write each step clearly enough that it can be duplicated by classmates to verify that Galileo was correct.

RECOMMENDED READING

Interested students can read a more detailed account of Galileo's life. They can report on some of the details that they find and how that book compares to the Fisher book the class read. Students can also read *Dragonwings* or another book about a scientist or technologist at work. Students can compare and contrast the problems, methods, influences, and successes of each. Suggest that students draw conclusions about the culture of these scientists and its view toward science and technology.

OTHER CONNECTIONS
ART/HISTORY

Have students investigate the Renaissance (fourteenth through seventeenth centuries) in Europe. Tell them that *renaissance* means "rebirth" and it was called this because of the rediscovery of the writings of the ancient Greeks and Romans. Suggest students find evidence of this rebirth in the book *Galileo.* Create cooperative learning groups to investigate other changes during the Renaissance. One group can concentrate on scientists and new scientific discoveries (i.e., Galileo, Kepler, and Newton) and their effects on technology. Another can research important technologies, such as the printing press, and how each changed life. Another group can investigate new forms and ideas in art. Other groups can investigate new political and religious ideas, such as various aspects of the Reformation and the growth of cities and countries. Still another group can report on the European settlement of the Americas. Students can share their findings with the class and together the class can create a master timeline.

MATH

Use the dates in the book to create, or have students create, a series of word problems. For example, one problem might ask students how long was it after Copernicus' book was published that Galileo was born? (1 year) You can also add dates for other people and events discussed, such as when Aristotle lived (384-322 b.c.), or when Sir Isaac Newton published the law of gravity (1687).

From *Science & Stories,* published by GoodYearBooks. Copyright © 1994 Hilarie N. Staton and Tara McCarthy.

LESSON 3

INVESTIGATING THE PLANETS

LITERATURE:
Journey to the Planets
Patricia Lauber (Crown Publishers, 1993)

SCIENCE UNDERSTANDING:
Each planet in our solar system has unique characteristics based on the matter of which it is made.

LITERARY GENRE:
Nonfiction

BOOK SUMMARY
In this book, Patricia Lauber summarizes many of the known characteristics of the planets in our solar system. She discusses the formation of each, its atmosphere, physical characteristics, core, and moons. For those planets with moons, pertinent information and pictures about the moons are also included. She describes how we know the facts, such as through the use of Earth-based instruments, satellites, or probes. All of the illustrations are photographs taken by these means. For all planets, Lauber discusses how they formed and are evolving. Although she includes many concepts, she makes them clear using a varied sentence structure and without a highly technical vocabulary.

PRE-READING
If you have not introduced space with the unit introductory activity (page 103), you might want to do so now.

1. Present and discuss a map or diagram of the solar system. Leave it visible so you and students can refer to it during the lesson. In order to give students a sense of the relative size of the solar system's planets, display the following without identifying the planets they represent: a beach ball (Sun), 2 grains of sand (Mercury and Pluto), two peas (Earth and Venus), a rice grain (Mars), a golf ball (Jupiter), a Ping Pong ball (Saturn), and two grapes (Uranus, Neptune). Tell students they are using a scale of 1 to 3,000,000,000 and using this scale, these items represent the planets in our solar system. Have them use the solar system map to guess which item represents which planet.

2. Once the planets are appropriately labeled, assign each planet to a small group of students. If students have the skills, write the first and second columns of the following chart on the chalkboard, and let them determine the meters for the third column (the correct answer is in parentheses). If students don't have the skills, place all three columns on the board.

Distance from the Sun	million kilometers	meters
Mercury	58	(19)
Venus	108	(36)
Earth	150	(50)
Mars	228	(76)
Jupiter	778	(259)
Saturn	1430	(477)
Uranus	2870	(967)
Neptune	4500	(1500)
Pluto	5900	(1970)

3. If you have enough available space outdoors, or a long local road, you can have students do a planet walk to better understand these distances. Using meter sticks and chalk, students can locate where each planet would be in their scale model showing the relative distances between the planets. They should be sure to have their "planet" (the item that represents its relative size) with them and try to see it from other vantage points in their "solar system." Other variations of this activity involve using larger items and going for a bus ride to identify the relative distances.

4. Hold up the book *Journey to the Planets* and flip through the pages while displaying random pictures. Identify these as photographs taken of the actual planets, not drawings or paintings. Identify the information in this book as recent scientific findings. Ask students how scientists get their pictures and information today.

BUILDING THE SCIENCE AND LITERATURE CONNECTION

1. Make a copy on the chalkboard or on chart paper of the chart on the Solar System Study Guide. You can add or delete items on the chart according to the level, interest, and prior knowledge of your students. As you read the first chapter to students, stop and discuss the information with students. Determine where on the chart the information should be placed. Be sure to discuss picture captions and the pictures themselves. When you have finished the chapter, discuss the final questions on the Study Guide, as they pertain to the earth. Add information to the chart as you read the book.

2. Read the second chapter, "A Star Is Born," so students understand its complex concepts. Discuss the main points as you go, relating the information to the first chapter, the students' prior knowledge, and the solar system map. Continue this procedure for the rest of the book.

3. Students can use the chart on the planets to write an essay comparing or describing some important characteristics of two or three planets. They should include the reasons why they believe people can or cannot live on that planet. Encourage students to use sentences with a variety of structures in each paragraph. Suggest students use peer editors from their group for editing and revision suggestions. Give peer editors some criteria to go on, such as clear scientific writing, accurate facts, and proper use of capitals. Students can share their completed essays by reading them aloud or creating a bulletin board or book.

EXTENDING THE SCIENCE

Activity 1. Interested students might like to do more research on one planet, alone or with a small group. Each group member or group could write and contribute a chapter about their planet for a class book about the planets.

Activity 2. Interested students can research recent space probes, their purpose, where they went, what happened to them, and what they found out. Include the Mariner, Pioneer, Viking, Voyager, and Magellan series of probes sent into orbit from the late 1960s until the present. Students can create posters with this information to share them with the class.

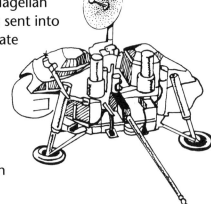

From *Science & Stories*, published by GoodYearBooks. Copyright © 1994 Hilarie N. Staton and Tara McCarthy.

Activity 3. Students can make an across-the-solar-system comparison chart of one or more basic scientific concepts, such as gravity, matter, atmosphere, etc. These charts can be used on a rotating series of bulletin boards about the planets or about specific scientific concepts.

EXTENDING THE LITERATURE

Activity 1. In order to get a better feel for the differences in nonfiction, fiction, and other types of writing, suggest students compare this text to a science text, novel, and encyclopedia. They can compare the sentence structures and phrases used, the interest level, clarity, enjoyability, ease of reading, and other factors. Have students draw some generalizations and state personal preferences about how these things affect their reading.

Activity 2. Suggest that students write tours of the solar system using the facts they know about the planets. They can pretend they are tour guides for a spacebus trip around the solar system who must describe the planets in an interesting and maybe humorous way. They can weave in background information about the planets, such as the origin of its name and date of discovery. These tours can be written specifically to introduce for younger students to the solar system. Encourage your students to perform these tours for science classes just learning about the planets.

OTHER CONNECTIONS
ART

Invite students to make illustrations of what they think it would be like on one of the planets in our solar system. They could do collages using various textures to represent the different types of materials and atmospheres. Or they could make drawings or paintings. Suggest they reread the chapter in the book to determine the types of colors, light, and textures they'll want represented.

MUSIC

Play Gustav Holst's *The Planets* for students without identifying which planet is the focus of each section. Then have students guess each planet. Encourage them to narrow their guesses by first reviewing descriptions of the planets, the myths about them, their namesakes (Mars, God of War), and how people thought about the planets in the past. Then have students try to match the planet to the movement as they listen again to the music.

MATH

Create or have students create a chart of specific characteristics of all the planets. These might include average distance from the sun, diameter, or time for one revolution. Students can then write a series of problems or graphs using these charts. They can trade problems with other students or have place them in a math center.

STUDY GUIDE TIPS

Answers will vary depending on the planet chosen. Some students do better by going from the particular to the general. Suggest that these students first find and record details about the planet (location, size, etc.), then go back and write the generalizations called for in the "What Scientists . . ." column. They will have found data for these generalizations as they searched out the details. Remind students to note the page numbers where they found the information.

Journey to the Planets

Name: _____ Date: _____

As you read each chapter in the book *Journey to the Planets*, think carefully about what you are reading. Use the information and your thoughts to fill in what scientists know, what they think they know, and what they'd want to know about each of the topics. Add some things you'd like to know about the topics too.

PLANET: _____

	What Scientists Know About the Planet	**What Scientists Think They Know**	**What Scientists Want to Know**	**What You'd Like to Know**
location:				
distance from the sun:				
size:				
axis:				
orbit:				
rotation:				
atmosphere:				
temperatures:				
surface features:				
changes that are happening:				
core:				
magnetic fields:				
moons:				
the most intriguing things about this planet:				

Give some examples of various states of matter on this planet.

_____

_____

_____

_____

_____

Give at least one example of motion on this planet.

_____

_____

_____

_____

_____

Give an example of energy on this planet.

_____

_____

_____

_____

_____

What words might be good ones to use to describe this planet?

_____

_____

_____

_____

_____

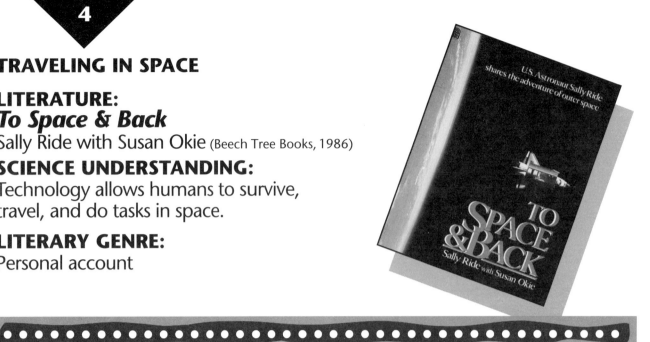

TRAVELING IN SPACE

LITERATURE:
To Space & Back
Sally Ride with Susan Okie (Beech Tree Books, 1986)

SCIENCE UNDERSTANDING:
Technology allows humans to survive, travel, and do tasks in space.

LITERARY GENRE:
Personal account

BOOK SUMMARY

This book is based on the personal experiences of NASA astronaut, Sally Ride. However, it does not stop at her experiences, but also describes life in the space shuttle in general. It is well illustrated with photographs of many shuttle missions and tries to answer the many questions people ask the astronauts. It has a fairly simple sentence structure, but does include technical words necessary to understand the subject matter.

In the first section, the astronauts begin their flight. What they see out the windows is clearly shown in a series of photographs of the earth and sunrise. The next section has to do with how the astronauts deal with weightlessness. Pictures show everything from eating on the ceiling to playing with a slinky without gravity. The next section describes the astronauts' food, as well as how they prepare and eat it. The astronauts catch scrambled eggs, juggle fruit, and capture floating pudding. Personal care problems, due to being without gravity, include keeping your arms down while you sleep, water globs floating in air, and going to the toilet. Technology has solved each of these in a unique way.

While in space, the astronauts spend most of their time doing a variety of jobs. Many require intense teamwork such as launching or recapturing and fixing satellites. Astronauts conduct scientific experiments in both the physical and biological sciences. Some astronauts get the exceptional experience of a spacewalk. In their bulky spacesuits and with the utmost care, they leave the ship and go into the void of space. The last section of the book is about reentry, landing, and returning to the gravity of the earth.

PRE-READING

If you have not introduced the concept of space to students, you might want to use the unit introductory activity (page 103) now.

1. Write the word *astronaut* on the chalkboard. Divide the word into its two parts and ask the student what they think each means. (*astro* is from the Greek *astron* for star and *naut* from the Greek *nautes* for sailor and *naus* for ship).

Encourage students to develop a meaning that combines these ideas into a definition. Ask students if they can name any astronauts, missions into space, etc. Encourage them to recall recent shuttle missions as well as earlier historic space and lunar missions.

2. Hold up the cover of *To Space and Back* and discuss the shuttle and Sally Ride, one of the authors. Point out to students that the cover copy contains a mistake. Strictly speaking, no one has ever gone into "outer space," as outer space refers to the universe beyond the solar system. Ask students where shuttle missions go (in orbit around the earth) and compare this to outer space.

3. Read to students pages 7 to 9 to further introduce Sally Ride, her credentials, and her purpose in writing this book. Have students predict the similarities and differences between this type of personal experience writing and scientific writing. You may also want to compare it with journal writing, which is even more personal and usually more immediate.

4. Display pages 10 and 11 from the book and discuss the shuttle's layout with students. Compare the limited amount of room for the astronauts with the spacious cargo room. Discuss where basic needs are met and how items are stored. Encourage students to look closely at the diagram and to ask questions about each area. Write the questions that no one can answer on a class chart that can be referred to as students read the book.

BUILDING THE SCIENCE AND LITERATURE CONNECTION

1. This is a good book for students to read out loud. You can provide a help with the technical vocabulary and concepts while they enjoy the easy language, interesting subject matter, and accessible information. Assign specific passages ahead of time and invite students to practice reading in pairs, so they can read their passage clearly, with appropri-

ate intonation and expression. Be sure to identify, define, and pronounce the unfamiliar and technical vocabulary. One student should also be responsible for discussing and describing pictures when they appear.

2. Students can devote most of one day to reading the book or it can be done in sections. Although no sections are given, the book easily divides into seven sections. Encourage the listening members of the class to answer the questions and then to ask other questions to clarify, classify, relate, and synthesize the information. Have them add the questions that cannot be answered to the class chart. Questions that are answered can be crossed off.

3. After the class has read the book, divide the students into small groups. Each group is going to present to the class a personal account of time on the shuttle. This account can be a skit, a journal, a story, letters, or a picture album with text. Groups base their events on the information in the book about tasks, technology, meeting personal needs and relationships. Suggest they refer back to the book to make their account accurate. Invite them to illustrate some of the technology using pictures or sculpture.

4. **Evaluation.** Invite each group to share its personal account with the class and to answer questions about it. Have the class evaluate how well the science is presented in each of the presentations.

EXTENDING THE SCIENCE

Activity 1. Students might like to investigate and compare the Soviet (now Russian) cosmonaut program with NASA's astronaut program. Students can create posters that proclaim the accomplishments of one program.

Activity 2. Students can research some experiments that have been done on the shuttle and compare the results with the same experiment done on the earth. Students can write newspaper articles or personal account magazine articles with their findings.

Activity 3. Students can investigate NASA's plans for future shuttle missions, a space station, space probes, and other missions to space. Encourage students to predict the type of training, technology, and skills necessary for the success of these missions. They can create a series of posters or ad campaigns informing people of the purpose of each mission.

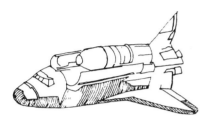

Activity 4. Students interested in space travel can research how astronauts are trained for the unusual conditions in space. Students can develop a brochure advertising the astronaut training program. It could list necessary qualifications and training procedures. Students might also investigate NASA's Space Camp for people not in the training program. If one of your students has been to NASA's Space Camp, have him or her report to the class.

EXTENDING THE LITERATURE
Activity 1. Interested students might like to write a travel journal from Sally Ride's or another astronaut's point of view, or for fun, from the perspective of a stowaway animal or inanimate object on the shuttle. Invite them to publish these accounts so others can read their stories.

RECOMMENDED READING
Students can read a biography, biographical article, or a personal account of another astronaut. Afterwards, they can write an essay comparing that person's ideas, experiences, and attitudes with those of Sally Ride's.

OTHER CONNECTIONS
SOCIAL STUDIES
Create an illustrated timeline of human space exploration. Encourage students to include both the Soviet (now Russian) and American accomplishments, possibly on a dual timeline for more recent years. Illustrations can include the spacecraft, people, or symbols of important missions.

DANCE
Create a dance to "space music." The movements can be based on the weightlessness astronauts encounter in space and the technology they must use to survive.

GEOGRAPHY
Many of the pictures of the earth in the book have captions that tell what part of the earth is visible. Have students locate the appropriate places on a globe and identify where a spacecraft would need to be to take each picture. Pictures from the earth and flat maps of the same place can be used for comparison.

From *Science & Stories*, published by GoodYearBooks. Copyright © 1994 Hilarie N. Staton and Tara McCarthy.

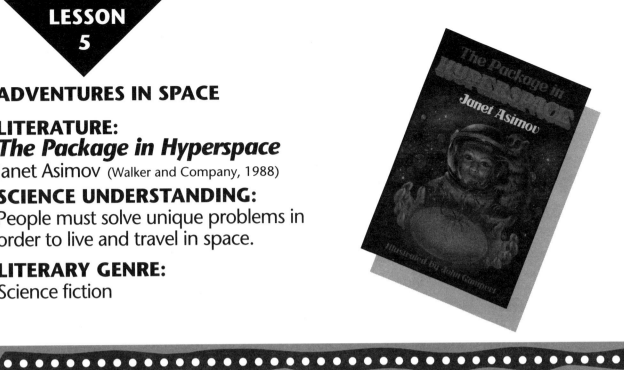

LESSON 5

ADVENTURES IN SPACE

LITERATURE:
The Package in Hyperspace
Janet Asimov (Walker and Company, 1988)

SCIENCE UNDERSTANDING:
People must solve unique problems in order to live and travel in space.

LITERARY GENRE:
Science fiction

BOOK SUMMARY

Ginnela, her younger brother Pete, and his pet, Lof, are trapped on a disabled spaceship, the Samson. They are traveling automatically through hyperspace and are unable to control the ship or to communicate with other people. An alien ship has crashed into the Samson and they can't communicate with its computer, either. With the help of a limited auxiliary computer on the Samson, they study their options. They deal with spacesuits, energy conservation, and limited supplies of food.

Twice Ginnela enters and investigates the alien ship only to be rescued by Pete. She brings back a small package, which turns out to be a music toy. This toy sings along with the children and Lof. As the time passes, the children become disheartened. This intensifies when the music toy locks into their computer, takes it over, and takes away their ability to communicate with it. Ginnela plays Beethoven's *Fifth Symphony* for courage and the music toy responds to it. Over and over they play it until suddenly, with the energy and food running out, the computer begins to communicate with them. However, they don't understand its colors, dots, dashes, and unintelligible sounds.

Eventually, the children realize the computer is using its knowledge of international communication symbols and Morse code to communicate. Slowly they realize the computer can understand their English and they quickly solve their food problem by having it turn on the food synthesizer. They use the few alien words they know and the music toy to return to the alien spaceship, where they must give themselves over to its computer to learn the alien language. At long last, after they have introduced the civilization they knew to the aliens, they realize that music is a universal language.

PRE-READING

If you have not introduced students to the concept of space and other words that relate to it, you might want to do the unit introductory activity (page 103) now.

1. Ask student what they think the term *science fiction* means. While accepting any reasonable answer, guide the students to the conclusion that it is fiction about the future that often uses real science as a basis for imaginary events, science, and technology. Ask students to recall television shows, movies, comic books, and stories they believe

are science fiction. Encourage them to differentiate between real science and the imaginary science in their examples.

2. Introduce the book and tell students that one problem with reading science fiction is that it often uses terms they may not be familiar with, such as hyperspace. Invite them to suggest meanings for the word. Then suggest that they suspend their final definition until they come across it in the book. Somewhere it will probably have a context from which they can infer its meaning. Warn them that they will encounter other words and ideas which will be unfamiliar, possibly completely made-up by the author. Ask what strategies students could use to deal with these terms.

BUILDING THE SCIENCE AND LITERATURE CONNECTION

1. This book is a good one to read aloud or to use as a reader's theater in either whole class or small-group settings. It is mostly dialogue, and although some words are hard, many of the concepts are quickly explained. If students read it in groups of three or four, each can have an assigned part and these parts can rotate for different chapters. Groups can discuss and answer the Study Guide questions, and the class can come together after each chapter. The answers to these Study Guide questions can be written or the questions can be used to guide class discussions. Be sure to discuss the science and events of the most complex chapters, such as Chapters 1, 3, 5, 7, 10, and 11. To ensure that students are not lost because of a lack of science understanding or because of the complex action, a summary is the first question for every chapter. The science chart at the end of the Study Guide can be done as a large class chart instead of as an individual or small group activity. More ideas can be added to it before the students do their final unit projects.

2. After the students have completed the book, the Study Guide, and a discussion of the book and its science, have them form new small groups. Assign or have each group choose one of the following problems or identify problems on their own:

- There is no atmosphere in space.
- There is no gravity away from a planet.
- Spaceships take a lot of energy to run.
- Computers only understand what they have been programmed to understand.
- People need food and air to survive.

After students read the problem, they should research and review the science behind it. Then have each group identify how the obstacle was overcome in the book and another way a science fiction author might solve it.

3. **Evaluation.** Have students write and practice skits using their solution and then share the skits and the science behind them with the class. The class can determine whether each group used science to create a believable and imaginative solution for the problem. They might rate several items, like those that follow, from 1 (very well done) to 5 (unclear or lacks thoroughness).

- The skit was based on correct science principles.
- The science in the skit was well explained.
- The skit was believable.
- The skit showed the use of imagination.
- The solution was one that could have been possible.

EXTENDING THE SCIENCE

Activity 1. Students might enjoy locating specific parts of the story and identifying the real laws and concepts that apply. They can illustrate the events and then label the aspects that fit specific laws. These illustrations can be displayed around the room.

Activity 2. Students might enjoy researching the items in the last column (Unknown Science) on their Study Guide chart to determine

From Science & Stories, published by GoodYearBooks. Copyright © 1994 Hilarie N. Staton and Tara McCarthy.

whether it is fictional or factual science, and the principles upon which it is based.

RECOMMENDED READING
Students who have read *To Space and Back* (Lesson 4) can identify the similarities and differences in real and imaginary space travel. They can create travel posters for each kind, emphasizing the differences in them.

EXTENDING THE LITERATURE
Activity. Students might enjoy writing newspaper or magazine articles that might have appeared after the children in the story returned to human civilization. These articles could include information about the aliens, the children's time with them, their trip, or their background.

ADDITIONAL READING
Students might enjoy reading other science fiction books about space travel or alien creatures. Note: There are not as many new books about space travel as old ones. If you have access to out of print books, check for books by Andre Norton, Robert Heinlein, or the Space Cadet series. Many recent books deal with aliens coming to the earth and how people react to them.

OTHER CONNECTIONS
ART
Invite students to illustrate parts of the book using various mediums. They might want to use dark material and glitter to illustrate the scene which shows Ginnela outside the ship or yarn to create Lof. Encourage them to display their art works around the room.

MUSIC
Besides playing Beethoven's *Fifth Symphony* for students, play other classical music that might inspire courage or transcend cultures. Show them the beginning of the movie *2001: A Space Odyssey* and discuss how the music complements and is a backdrop for the action.

SOCIAL STUDIES
Have students plan a new society on a planet or in a long distance space ship. They can examine how the society will be governed, how jobs and schooling will be assigned, how basic and more casual needs will be met, and what the leisure and recreational activities will be. Students can create graphs or diagrams with the pertinent information as well as skits, stories, or journals to share the information in a lively way with the class.

1. Suggest that students write chapter summaries on separate sheets of paper and keep them in sequence in a folder. Use the summaries for general review or as a resource for locating specific information in the book.

2. Remind students to write the number of the page on which they find the answer to a question. This is a handy reference strategy should differences of opinion or recollection arise during general class discussions.

3. Although student answers will vary, all students should come away with the realization that much of the science in the story was based on fact. The science that the author made up had an internal logic that made it seem real. The final chart will vary depending on students' knowledge, but the following list is of actual, not fictional scientific devices. Some of the student might be surprised to find that these facts are real.

4. Actual scientific devices: voice-controlled computers, air being sucked into space, duct systems, storage cells, life support systems, artificial gravity, airlock, float in space, magnetized boots, intercom, spacesuit, air tester on spacesuit, locks that open with fingers, touch-in-sequence locks, sculptures that move with light and sound, computer with sensors to identify an object, and larger computers giving information to smaller computers. A few fictional science devices, like a learning device that goes directly from the computer to the brain, are under development, but not yet a reality.

From *Science & Stories*, published by GoodYearBooks. Copyright © 1994 Hilarie N. Staton and Tara McCarthy.

The Package in Hyperspace

Name:_____ Date:_____

After you read each chapter, answer the questions below.

Chapter 1. Summarize this chapter in your own words. Then answer these questions.

a. What problems did Ginnela and Pete face in this chapter?

b. How did they attempt to solve them?

c. From the context, explain what a "transporter room" is.

d. Use the chart at the end of the Study Guide to categorize the following items: transporter room, hyperjumps, loffo, hyperspace, voice-controlled computers, and air being sucked into space.

Chapter 2. Summarize this chapter in your own words. Then answer these questions.

a. Ginnela and Pete realize that they have a serious problem. What factors make their problem very serious?

b. What attempts do they make to try and solve their problems?

c. From the context, explain something about hyperspace and hyperjumps.

d. Use the chart at the end of the Study Guide to categorize the following items: duct system, hycom, and a computer with emotions.

Chapter 3. Summarize this chapter in your own words. Then answer these questions.

a. Ginnela and Pete realize they have a problem with the energy system on the ship. List the things on board ship that run on energy. What is their problem and how do they try to solve it?

b. From the context, explain something about artificial gravity and life support systems.

c. Use the chart at the end of the Study Guide to categorize the following items: storage cells, life support systems, food synthesizer, artificial gravity, protective field, and animals who breathe sulfur air.

Chapter 4. Summarize this chapter in your own words. Then answer these questions.

a. What personality traits do you think Ginnela and Pete have that will help them survive this adventure?

b. Predict how they might help each other to survive this adventure.

From *Science & Stories*, published by GoodYearBooks. Copyright © 1994 Hilarie N. Staton and Tara McCarthy.

Chapter 5. Summarize this chapter in your own words. Then answer these questions.

a. Why do you think Ginnela took the action she did? What problems did her actions cause?

b. Predict what will happen next.

c. Identify three scientific ideas, like gravity, that have played a part in this story so far.

d. Use the chart at the end of the Study Guide to categorize the following items: airlock, float in space, magnetized boots, intercom, spacesuit, and an air tester on the suit.

Chapter 6. Summarize this chapter in your own words. Then answer these questions.

a. What problems did Ginnela have while in the alien spaceship?

b. What you think the purpose of the bubble-filled room and the package are?

c. Use the chart at the end of the Study Guide to categorize the following items: locks that open with fingers and touch-in-sequence locks.

Chapter 7. Summarize this chapter in your own words. Then answer these questions.

a. What problems do you think the package could cause or solve?

b. Use the chart at the end of the Study Guide to categorize the following items: sculpture that moves with light and sound and a computer with sensors to identify an object.

Chapter 8. Summarize this chapter in your own words. Then answer these questions.

a. How does the Beethoven music cube help Ginnela?

b. What problem does the music toy cause and how do Ginnela and Pete try to solve it?

c. From the context, what do you think the Laws of Robotics are?

d. Predict what you think will happen next.

e. Use the chart at the end of the Study Guide to categorize the following items: larger computer giving information to smaller computer and music cubes.

Chapter 9. Summarize this chapter in your own words. Then answer these questions.

a. What problems do the children need to solve during the chapter and how do they solve them?

b. Predict what you think will happen next.

c. Use the chart at the end of the Study Guide to categorize the following items: sulfur air and a metal burner in space.

Chapter 10. Summarize this chapter in your own words. Then answer these questions.

a. Why do you think the music toy reacted to the music of Beethoven as it did?

b. What new problems do the children have to solve and how do they try to solve them?

c. Using the context of the book, in what ways do people communicate?

From *Science & Stories*, published by GoodYearBooks. Copyright © 1994 Hilarie N. Staton and Tara McCarthy.

d. Predict what you think will happen next.

e. Use the chart at the end of the Study Guide to categorize the following items: miniantigrav, Morse code, and aliens in the universe.

Chapter 11. Summarize this chapter in your own words. Then answer these questions.

a. Part of the story is missing and you must supply it for yourself. Think about the characters, technology, and the final events. Then explain what you think happened from the time Ginnela "gave in" to the alien's computer until they reached the house of their aunt or uncle.

b. Use the chart at the end of the Study Guide to categorize the following items: mind link and a learning device direct from computer to brain.

Real and Imaginary Science

Think about the items listed on the study guide and decide which of the following categories they best fit into.

Real Science (if it is based on science facts we know about today)

Fictional Science (if it is science that the author is making up)

Unknown Science (if you don't know enough about this topic yet)

Write each item under the best heading.

REAL SCIENCE	FICTIONAL SCIENCE	UNKNOWN SCIENCE

Additional Resources

RECOMMENDED BOOKS AND SOFTWARE FOR STUDENTS

The book titles and software titles are organized by the five units in *Science & Stories 4-6*.

THE OCEAN
Books

Ancona, George. *Turtle Watch.* (Macmillan, 1987).

Anton, Tina. *Sharks, Sharks, Sharks.* (Raintree, 1989).

Ashby, Ruth. *Jane Goodall's Animal World: Sea Otters.* (Aladdin, 1990).

Blair, Carvel Hall. *Exploring the Sea: Oceanography Today.* (Random House, 1986).

Bunting, Eve. *The Giant Squid.* (Messner, 1981).

The Cousteau Society. *Corals, The Seas' Great Builders.* (Simon & Schuster, 1991).

Crump, Donald J. *Amazing Animals of the Sea.* (National Geographic, 1981).

Daegling, Mary. *Monster Seaweeds: The Story of the Giant Kelps.* (Dillon, 1986).

Doris, Ellen. *Marine Biology.* (Thomas & Hudson, 1993).

Gilbreath, Alice. *River in the Ocean: The Story of the Gulf Stream.* (Dillon, 1986).

Lavies, Bianca. *The Atlantic Salmon.* (Dutton, 1992).

O'Dell, Scott. *Island of the Blue Dolphins.* (Houghton Mifflin, 1960).

Mallory, Kenneth, and Conley, Andrea. *Rescue of the Stranded Whales.* (Simon & Schuster, 1989).

Papastavrou, Vassili. *Whales and Dolphins.* (Bookwright, 1991).

Patent, Dorothy Hinshaw. *Dolphins and Porpoises.* (Holiday, 1987).

Russell, Solveig Paulson. *What's Under the Sea?* (Abingdon, 1982).

Settle, Mary Lee. *Water World.* (Lodestar, 1984).

Seymour, Peter. *What Lives in the Sea?* (Macmillan, 1985).

Simon, Seymour. *Oceans.* (Morrow, 1990).

Simon, Seymour. Whales. Crowell, 1989.

Stolz, Mary. *Night of Ghosts and Hermits: Nocturnal Life on the Seashore.* (Harcourt, 1985).

Software

A Field Trip into the Sea. Wings for Learning, 1600 Green Hills Rd. P.O. Box 660002, Scotts Valley, CA 95067. Macintosh, or Apple II.59 p. manual; a book, The Kelp Forest. Marine habitat including shore, underwater, and surface organisms.

Eco-Adventures: The Oceans. Chariot Software Group, 3659 India St., Number 100, San Diego, CA 92103. Macintosh, or IBM AT or compatible. 44 p. manual, poster. Students score points on an oceanic mission to discover facts and sources of pollution.

Eco Quest I: The Search for Setus. Sierra On-Line, Inc. P.O. Box 978, Oakhurst, CA 93644.IBM, Atari, Amiga, or Macinotsh. 32 p. manual, book. Adam and a dolphin attempt to save the dolphin's underwater home through problem solving and logic oriented around ecological tasks.

PATTERNS OF CHANGE
Books

Ames, Gerald, and Wyler, Rose. *The Story of the Ice Age.* (Harper, 1956).

Bain, Ian. *Mountains and Earth Movements.* (Franklin Watts, 1984).

Branley, Franklyn M. *What Happened to the Dinosaurs?* (Harper, 1989).

Clark, Margaret Goff. *The Vanishing Manatee.* (Dutton, 1990).

Dowden, Anne Ophelia. *The Blossom on the Bough: A Book of Trees.* (Harper, 1978).

Durea, Olivier. *Skara Brae: The Story of a Prehistoric Village.* (Holiday, 1986).

Eldredge, Gregory, and Eldredge, Douglas. *The Fossil Factory.* (Addison-Wesley, 1989).

Facklam, Margery. *And Then There Was One: The Mysteries of Extinction.* (Little, Brown, 1990).

Fradin, Dennis B. *Droughts.* (Childrens Press, 1983).

Gallant, Roy A. *Before the Sun Dies: The Story of Evolution.* (Macmillan, 1989).

Gallant, Roy A. *Fossils.* (Franklin Watts, 1986).

George, Jean Craighead. *13 Moons* Series. (HarperCollins).

Horner, John R., and Lessem, Don. *Digging Up Tyrannosuarus Rex.* (Crown, 1992).

Lambert, David, and Hardy, Ralph. *Weather and Its Work.* (Facts on File, 1984).

Lauber, Patricia. *Volcano: The Eruption and Healing of Mount St. Helens.* (Bradbury, 1986).

Lindsay, Mary, ed. *The Visual Dictionary of Plants.* (Dorling, 1992).

McGowen, Tom. *Album of Prehistoric Man.* (Macmillan, 1975).

Merriman, Nick. *Early Humans.* (Knopf, 1989).

Muller, Jorg. *The Changing Countryside.* (Macmillan, 1986).

Scott, Jack Denton. *Alligator.* (Putnam, 1984).

Sigford, Ann E. *Tall Grass and Trouble: A Story of Environmental Action.* (Dillon, 1978).

Simon, Seymour. *Storms.* (Morrow, 1989).

Steele, William O. *Talking Bones: Secrets of Indian Mound Builders.* (Harper, 1978).

Stone, Lynn. *Alligators and Crocodiles.* (Children's Press, 1989).

Wyler, Rose. *Raindrop and Raindrop.* (Messner, 1989).

Yolen, Jane. *Ring of Earth.* (Harcourt, 1986).

Software

Sprout. Abracadata, P.O. Box 2440, Eugene OR 97402. Macintosh and IBM PC/XT/AT. 167 p. manual. Students plan and plant a vegetable garden according to planting conditions, climate, and plant needs.

Genetics and Heredity. Educational Activities, P.O. Box 392, Freeport, NY 11520. Apple, IBM, Tandy. 18 p. manual. Four lessons (c. 12-25 minutes in length) take students through Mendel's laws and genotype vs. phenotype.

ECOSYSTEMS
Books

Ahlstrom, Mark. *The Coyote.* (Crestwood, 1985).

Batten, Mary. *The Tropical Forest.* (Harper, 1973).

Brown, Mary Barrett. *Wings Along the Waterway.* (Orchard, 1992).

Browne, Tom. *Rivers and People.* (Silver, 1982).

Carr, Terry. *Spill! The Story of the Exxon Valdez.* (Watts, 1991).

Cherry, Lynne. *A River Ran Wild.* (Harcourt, 1992).

Fleischman, Paul. *Joyful Noise: Poems for Two Voices.* (Harper, 1988).

Fodor, R.V. *Earth Afire! Volcanoes and Their Activity.* (Morrow, 1981).

Forsyth, Adrian. *Journey Through a Tropical Jungle.* (Simon & Schuster, 1989).

George, Jean Craighead. *One Day in the Alpine Tundra.* (Harper, 1984).

Hammer, Trudy J. *Water Resources.* (Franklin Watts, 1985).

Hare, Tony. *Vanishing Habitats.* (Gloucester, 1991).

Johnson, Rebecca. *The Great Barrier Reef: A Living Laboratory.* (Lerner, 1991).

Kastner, Joseph. *John James Audubon.* (Abrams, 1992).

Kudlinski, Kathleen V. *Rachel Carson: Pioneer of Ecology.* (Viking, 1988).

Lambert, David. *Vegetation.* (Franklin Watts, 1984).

Lampton, Christopher. *Tidal Wave.* (Millbrook, 1992).

Larrick, Nancy, ed. *Room for Me and a Mountain Lion: Poetry of Open Spaces.* (Evans, 1974).

O'Dell, Scott. *Island of the Blue Dolphins.* (Houghton Mifflin, 1960).

Parker, Steve. *Pond and River.* (Knopf, 1988).

Rennicke, Jeff. *The Bears of Alaska in Life and Legend.* (Roberts Rinehart, 1987).

Schwartz, David M. *The Hidden Life of the Meadow.* (Crown, 1988).

Siebert, Diane. *Mojave.* (Harper, 1988).

Silverstein, Alvin, and Silverstein, Virginia. *Life in a Tidal Pool.* (Little, 1990).

Software

Ecosystem Lab. Galileo Software, Inc., 2410 Springwagon Ln., Austin, TX 78728. IBM or compatibles. 92 p. guide. Students set up ecosystems for species, using variables of mobility, average life span, and initial population.

Clearwater Detectives. MECC, 6160 Summitt Dr. N., Minneapolis, MN 55430. Apple. 43 p. manual. Students investigate water contaminants, find pollution sources, and recommend actions.

EcoVision. Houghton Mifflin, One Beacon St., Boston, MA 02108. Apple II GS. 143 p.

teacher's guide, 26 p. user's guide, two activity books. Students investigate four ecosystems using common principles.

TECHNOLOGY
Books

Bendick, Jeanne. *Eureka! It's a Television* and *Eureka! It's a Telephone.* (Millbrook, 1993).

Cooper, Chris, and Insley, Jane. *How Does it Work?* (Facts on File, 1986).

Darling, David J. *Robots and the Intelligent Computer.* (Dillon, 1986).

Fisher, Leonard Everett. *The Great Wall of China.* (Macmillan, 1986).

Fisher, Leonard Everett. *Tracks Across America: The Story of the American Railroad.* (Holiday, 1992).

Folsom, Michael, and Folsom, Marcia. *The Macmillan Book of How Things Work.* (Macmillan, 1987).

Garrison, Webb. *Why Didn't I Think of That? From Alarm Clocks to Zippers.* (Prentice Hall, 1977).

Giblin, James Cross. *The Skyscraper Book.* (Harper, 1981).

Goldberg, Rube. *The Best of Rube Goldberg.* (Prentice Hall, 1979).

Greene, Laura. *Computer Pioneers.* (Franklin Watts, 1985).

Laithwaite, Eric. *Using Materials.* (Franklin Watts, 1988).

Lambert, Mark. *Living in the Future.* (Franklin Watts, 1986).

Lasky, Kathryn. *The Weaver's Gift.* (Warne, 1981).

Macaulay, David. *Underground.* (Houghton Mifflin, 1976).

Saunders, Rupert. *Balloon Voyage.* (Rourke, 1988).

Smith, Elizabeth Simpson. *Cloth.* (Walker, 1985).

Sobol, Donald J. *The Wright Brothers at Kitty Hawk.* (Scholastic, 1987).

Sullivan, George. *Famous Blimps and Airships.* (Putnam, 1988).

Weiss, Harvey. *Shelters: From Tepee to Igloo.* (Harper, 1988).

SPACE
Books

Asimov, Isaac. *Environments Out There.* (Harper, 1967).

Barrett, N.S. *Astronauts.* (Franklin Watts, 1985).

Bean, Alan. *My Life as an Astronaut.* (Pocket paper, 1988).

Billings, Charlene W. *Christa McAuliffe: Pioneer Space Teacher.* (Enslow, 1986).

Branley, Franklyn M. *Mysteries of Life on Earth and Beyond.* (Dutton, 1987).

Branley, Franklyn M. *Mysteries of the Universe.* (Lodestar, 1984).

Briggs, Carole S. *Women in Space.* (Lerner, 1988).

Darling, David J. *The Galaxies: Cities of Stars.* (Dillon, 1985).

Gallant, Roy. *The Macmillan Book of Astronomy.* (Macmillan, 1986).

Gunston, Bill. *Aircraft.* (Franklin Watts, 1986).

Hamilton, Virginia. *In the Beginning: Creation Stories from Around the World.* (Harcourt, 1988).

Lampton, Christopher. *Astronomy: From Copernicus to the Space Telescope.* (Franklin Watts, 1987).

Lauber, Patricia. *Voyagers from Space: Meteors and Meteorites.* (Harper, 1989).

Maurer, Richard. *The Nova Space Explorer's Guide: Where to Go and What to See.* (Crown, 1986).

McPhee, Penelope, and McPhee, Raymond. *Your Future in Space: The U.S. Space Camp Training Program.* (Crown, 1986).

Moskin, Marietta. *Sky Dragons and Flaming Swords: The Story of Eclipses, Comets, and Other Strange Happenings in the Skies.* (Walker, 1985).

Weiss, Malcolm E. *Sky Watchers of Ages Past.* (Houghton Mifflin, 1982).

Software

Sky Travel—Mac. William K. Bradford, 310 School St., Acton, MA 01720. Macintosh 512 or later. 25 p. manual. A planetarium program through which students can view the night sky as it was 10,000 years ago or far into the future.

Rocket Factory. MECC, 6160 Summitt Dr. N., Minneapolis, MN 55430. Apple. 93 p. manual. Students combine components to launch rockets, adjust payloads, explore principles of force and motion.

Recommended Professional Materials

Abruscato, Joe, and Hassard, Jack. *The Whole Cosmos Catalogue of Science Activities.* (GoodYearBooks, 1991).

Allman, A. S., and Koop, O.W. *Environmenal Education: Guideline Activities for Children and Youth.* (Merrill, 1976).

Caduto, Michael J., and Bruchac, Joseph. *Keepers of the Animals.* (Fulcrum, 1991).

Caduto, Michael J., and Bruchac, Joseph. *Keepers of the Earth.* (Fulcrum, 1989).

Cannon, Robert L., and Banks, Michael. *The Rocket Book: A Guide to Building and Launching Model Rockets for Teachers and Students of the Space Age.* (Prentice Hall, 1985).

Farndon, John. *How the Earth Works: 100 Ways Parents and Kids Can Share the Secrets of the Earth.* (Reader's Digest, 1992).

Moutran, Julia Spencer. *Elementary Science Activities for All Seasons.* (Simon & Schuster, 1990).

Project Wild and Project Aquatic. Western Regional Environmental Council, P.O. Box 18060, Boulder, CO 80308-8060.

Richardson, Elwyn. *In the Early World.* (New Zealand Council for Educational Research, 1964).

Schmidt, V., and Rockcastle, V. *Teaching Science with Everyday Things.* (McGraw-Hill, 1968).

Science and Children. Published eight times a year by the National Science Teachers Association, Washington, D.C.

Stein, Sara. *The Evolution Book.* (Workman, 1986).

Tchudi, Stephen. *Probing the Unknown: From Myth to Science.* (Macmillan, 1990).

The Visible Universe. Time-Life Book Editors. (Time Life Books, 1990).

Water, Precious Water: Project AIMS; A Collection of Elementary Water Activities. AIMS Education Foundation, P.O. Box 776, Fresno, CA 93747.